Titles in the series

www.amazingstoriesbooks.com

LATE-BREAKING
AMAZING STORIES™

WRONGFULLY ACCUSED

Innocent people on death row

by Nora Rock

PUBLISHED BY ALTITUDE PUBLISHING LTD.
1500 Railway Avenue, Canmore, Alberta T1W 1P6
www.amazingstoriesbooks.com
1-800-957-6888

Extreme care has been taken to ensure that the information contained in this book is accurate and up to date at the time of printing. However, neither the author nor the publisher is responsible for errors, omissions, loss of income, or anything else that may result from the information contained in this book.

All web site URLs mentioned in this book were correct at the time of printing. The publisher is not responsible for the content of external web sites or changes that may have occurred since publication.

In order to make this book as universal as possible, all currency is shown in U.S. dollars.

Publisher	Stephen Hutchings
Associate Publisher	Kara Turner
Canadian Editors	Ros Penty and Frances Purslow
U.S. Editor	Julian S. Martin
Charts	Scott Dutton

We acknowledge the financial support of the Government of Canada through the Book Publishing Industry Development Program (BPIDP) for our publishing activities.

ALTITUDE GREENTREE PROGRAM
Altitude Publishing will plant twice as many trees as were used in the manufacturing of this product.

Cataloging in Publication Data
Rock, Nora, 1968-
    Wrongfully accused / Nora Rock. -- Canadian ed.

(Late breaking amazing stories)
Includes bibliographical references.
ISBN 1-55265-311-0 (American mass market edition)
ISBN 1-55439-513-5 (Canadian mass market edition)

    1. Death row. 2. Judicial error. 3. Prisoners. I. Title. II. Series.

HV6515.R62 2006a	364.66	C2006-900678-4 (U.S.)
HV6515.R62 2006	364.66	C2006-900677-6 (Cdn.)

In Canada, Amazing Stories® is a registered trademark of Altitude Publishing Canada Ltd. An application for the same trademark is pending in the U.S.

Printed and bound in Canada by Friesens
2 4 6 8 9 7 5 3 1

"I am a human being."

Last words of David Lawson, executed in 1994

"You always lose some soldiers in any war."

Senator David Jaye, R-Washington Township

CONTENTS

Wallace Conners (left), photographed July 2005. Although Conners was shot he was never contacted by the defense or the prosecution following the drive-by shooting in 1980 for which Larry Griffin was convicted and later executed. For more on the story, see Chapter 1.

(Photo: AP Photo/James A. Finley)

Former Illinois governor George Ryan announces a moratorium on state executions January 31, 2000. For more on the story, see page 134.

(Photo: AP Photo/Stephen J. Carrera)

Luis Diaz, center, with his sons and his lawyer Barry Scheck, far right, is freed from prison August 3, 2005, in Miami, Florida. DNA evidence cleared him of the rape charges that he had served 26 years in prison for. For more on Barry Scheck's work, see Chapter 4.

(Photo: AP Photo/J. Pat Carter)

Sister Helen Prejean, the author of *Dead Man Walking*, photographed in 1996, is a champion of the innocent. For more on Sister Prejean, see page 147.

(Photo: AP Photo/ Richmond Times-Dispatch, Don Long)

This undated photo shows Kenneth Lee Boyd, the 1,000th person to be executed in the United States. Boyd was convicted in the March 1988 shooting deaths of his estranged wife and her father. He was executed December 2, 2005, in North Carolina.
(Photo: AP Photo/North Carolina Department of Correction)

Shawn Humphries, the 1,001st person to be executed in the United States, is shown in this undated photo. He was executed December 2, 2005, in South Carolina.
(Photo: AP Photo/ S.C. Dept. of Correction)

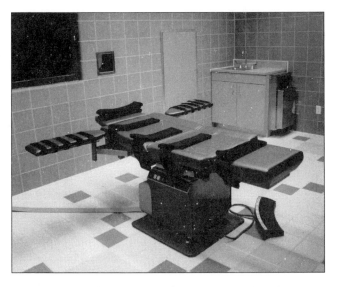

The death chamber at the U.S. Penitentiary in
Terre Haute, Indiana, shown in this April 1995 photo,
is the only federal death chamber in the United States,
and is equipped for lethal injection. Oklahoma City
bomber Timothy McVeigh was executed
in this facility June 11, 2001.
(Photo: AP Photo/Chuck Robinson)

CHAPTER 1

Two Stories

For his last meal before his November 2004 execution, Texas gunman Frederick Patrick McWilliams ordered six fried chicken breasts with ketchup, french fries, six-layer lasagna, six egg rolls, shrimp fried rice and soy sauce, six chimichangas with melted cheese and salsa, six slices of turkey with liver and gizzard dressing, dirty rice, cranberry sauce, and six lemonades with extra sugar.

McWilliams had been sentenced to death after admitting to the point-blank range shooting of a carjacking victim.

At the other end of the spectrum is Larry Griffin, who was also on death row for a shooting—in his case, a 1980 drive-by attack on a drug dealer in a crime-ridden neighborhood in St. Louis, Missouri. On the eve of his June 21, 1995, execution, when asked what he would like for his last meal. Larry, who had never wavered in his protests of innocence, ordered bread and water.

* * *

Ten years after Griffin's execution, on June 10, 2005, the National Association for the Advancement of Colored People (NAACP) released the report of its investigation into his case. The report, prepared by University of Michigan law professor Samuel Gross, raised questions that point to Griffin's innocence of the crime for which he'd been sentenced.

Faced with significant pressure from Gross, the NAACP, a Missouri congressman, and even some relatives of Griffin's alleged victim, top St. Louis prosecutor Jennifer Joyce agreed to re-open the investigation into the 1980 shooting. If the new investigation exonerates Griffin, he will be the first American officially proven to have been executed while innocent.

EXECUTION OF INNOCENTS

There is no record of an official, posthumous exoneration of a prisoner who received the death penalty in the United States. However, research studies suggest that the United States has executed plenty of innocents: according to one well-known report (Radelet, Bedau, and Putnam, 1994) *at least* 23 such executions occurred between the turn of the 20th century and 1984.

* * *

Today, a tidy row of newer townhouses occupies the corner of Olive and Sarah Street in St. Louis. In 1980, however, the corner was part of what was known as "the Stroll." Boarded-up houses and shops formed the backdrop for transactions involving sex, alcohol, and drugs. A short walk away on Olive, a methadone clinic catered to heroin addicts.

The neighborhood was overwhelmingly black, so much so that critics would later challenge the testimony of a white witness in Larry's case because no white man could have escaped notice—or harm—on the Stroll. Had a white man been on the street corner at the time of the drive-by shooting that put Larry on death row, said one witness, "He would have been shot, just like everyone else."

The fortunes—and safety—of the Stroll's black youth were determined by their affiliations in the local drug trade. At the time, dealers such as Dennis Griffin, Larry's older brother, and Quintin Moss, the 19-year-old murder victim, dominated that trade.

In the winter of 1979–1980, Dennis Griffin was murdered. The residents of the Stroll widely believed that Quintin Moss had done the killing;

Moss had been arrested, and then released due to a lack of evidence.

It was also common knowledge that as a result of the Dennis Griffin murder, a "contract" was outstanding for Moss's execution. Moss's sisters, Patricia and Sherry, had already urged him to leave St. Louis. A few weeks before he was murdered, Moss survived a shooting attempt on the same street corner on which he would eventually be killed. Police investigating that attempt pulled over a car; Larry Griffin was in the passenger seat and his cousin Reggie Griffin was driving. After a fruitless search for weapons, the young men were allowed to drive away. Reggie, but not Larry, was a member of Dennis Griffin's drug-trafficking gang.

On June 26, 1980, Quintin Moss was selling drugs near the corner of Olive and Sarah when a 1968 Chevy Impala drove slowly south on Sarah. When the car reached the spot where Moss stood, two shooters—one in the front passenger seat and the other in a rear seat—leaned out the window, guns at the ready. Moss was hit 13 times and fell to the ground. A 14th shot missed Moss and hit a passerby—Wallace Conners—in the buttocks. Conners fled eastward along Olive before collapsing onto the pavement.

What happened next is a matter of much dispute.

When the case went to trial, the prosecution introduced its star witness. Robert Fitzgerald had been relocated to St. Louis from Boston under the federal Witness Protection Program. He was staying in a hotel in St. Louis at the time of the shooting.

According to police, Fitzgerald came to their attention as a witness when he rushed to Quintin Moss's side and tried to take the dead man's pulse. He testified that he spoke with the first police officer on the scene, told the officer the license plate number of the car, and could identify the shooter. Fitzgerald testified that he had been stranded on the corner, just a few feet away from the shooting, because his car battery had died; he was watching over his friend's young daughter while the friend went to buy a replacement battery.

Fitzgerald also testified to having been taken to the police station, where he identified Larry Griffin from a photo array (he later changed his testimony and said he was shown only one photo: Larry's). As he was driven back to his hotel in the police cruiser, he identified the shooters' car.

Despite his extensive criminal record and his reputation as a snitch and a liar, Fitzgerald's testimony was the nail in Larry Griffin's coffin. The state obtained a conviction in 1981, and Larry was executed 14 years later.

The murder is now 25 years old, and Larry Griffin has been dead for over a decade. Normally, a death-row prisoner would be long forgotten, but rumors about Larry's case persist.

For one thing, no one else who witnessed the crime remembers having seen a person— let alone a white man in the very black Stroll neighborhood—bent over Moss's body before police arrived. No one saw a white man stranded near a broken-down car. No one saw a car at all. And although they both witnessed the shooting, neither Wallace Conners (the other shooting victim), nor Patricia Mason (Quintin Moss's sister) testified for the prosecution at the trial.

When questioned years later by investigators, Conners explained that had he been called to testify, he would have told the court that he'd seen the front-seat shooter, and that it wasn't Larry Griffin. Conners knew Griffin from the neighborhood. He was certain that at the time of the shooting, Larry Griffin was not in the shooters' car at all.

Another witness that NAACP investigators focused on in their efforts to re-open the case was Michael Ruggieri, the police officer to first arrive on the scene. Although Ruggieri's testimony at trial had been consistent with Robert Fitzgerald's—that Fitzgerald had been bent over Moss's body when Ruggieri showed up—there was no mention of Fitzgerald, or any parked car, or any license plate number from the shooters' car in Ruggieri's notes made at the scene of the crime.

When NAACP investigators interviewed Ruggieri, his account of the incident differed markedly from his testimony at trial. What he said was more consistent with his written notes. He was emphatic that there was no parked car at the scene, and he denied having been given the shooters' license plate number by anybody. This detail is confirmed by another officer—Sergeant Anthony Pona—who is certain that the license plate number was not available at the crime scene (if it had been, it would have been communicated over the radio, and written in Ruggieri's notes). Pona told the investigators that homicide detectives obtained the license plate number later.

Ruggieri did remember a white male coming up to Quintin's body later, after police had arrived. When questioned, the man replied, "I didn't see nuthin'."

Rumors in the community about the June 26, 1980, shooting point the finger not at Larry Griffin, but at three other men: Larry's cousin Reggie Griffin and two Ronnies—Ronnie Thomas-Bey and Ronnie Parker. NAACP investigators interviewed Jerry Lewis-Bey, Ronnie Thomas-Bey's cousin. At the time of the interview, Jerry was serving a sentence of life without parole for his involvement in a famous St. Louis crime—the Moorish Science Temple case. He told investigators that, upon returning to St. Louis from Montreal where he had seen a boxing match, he'd learned that his cousin Ronnie had been arrested for the drive-by shooting of Quintin Moss, but was later released. Jerry Lewis-Bey told investigators that at the time of the killing, Ronnie Parker was driving, Ronnie Thomas-Bey was in the front passenger seat, and Reggie Griffin was in the back seat. Larry Griffin was not involved. "Everyone back then knew that this was the way it went down," said Jerry Lewis-Bey. "It was gospel."

* * *

John Thompson was luckier than Larry. Though he, too, was sent to death row in his early 20s and languished there for many years, the Louisiana native is now a free man. In December 2003, John and his wife, Laverne, whom he met in elementary school and married not long after his May 2003 release from prison, took possession of a modest New Orleans house. Habitat for Humanity, a charitable organization dedicated to building homes for the needy, had built the house for them.

John, now 40, and Laverne have struggled financially since his release from prison. But in comparison to most long-term prison inmates, John is doing fine. On the Monday after his Friday release, he started work at the Center for Equal Justice, an organization that had been instrumental in finding him the unlikely counsel—a pair of Philadelphia commercial and employment litigators—who got him off death row.

Adjusting to life outside penitentiary walls is so difficult that many long-timers soon find themselves in trouble with the law and incarcerated again. Prisoners are typically released with just the clothes on their backs and a miniscule sum of money—$100 is common. But John was lucky in that he had a support network on the outside. Nathaniel Williams Sr., the maternal grandfather of John's younger son, John Jr., had followed the case closely over the years, and had provided a strong role model for John Jr., who was just a toddler when John Sr. was sentenced. Old friends and neighbors believed in John, despite his 18 years in prison. When he got out of prison, John was welcomed into his new wife's church.

* * *

Like many of the young men in his rough New Orleans childhood neighborhood, John hadn't always been a straight arrow. He dropped out of

school to care for the two sons he'd fathered before his 18th birthday. While his girlfriend (and
John Jr.'s mother, Denise Williams) attended
school and worked part-time, John developed a
reputation as a club-hopper and a drug dealer
on the streets of New Orleans.

On December 6, 1984, on those same
streets, a robber fatally shot a 34-year-old hotel
executive named Raymond Liuzza Jr., near his
apartment building.

The robber demanded a gold ring Liuzza
was wearing. Liuzza also offered his wallet and
watch to escape being killed, but he was shot
anyway. "Why did he have to shoot me?" the dying man asked of the police officer who leaned
over his body at the scene. The officer had arrived too late to spot the shooter.

But at least one person claimed to have
seen the whole thing. Sheri Hartman Kelly fled
New Orleans a month after the shooting. When
she was tracked down years later by Thompson's defense team, Kelly told investigators that

she had seen the shooting from her apartment balcony. The shooter, she said, was a muscular man with short hair. At the time of the shooting, John Thompson was slim and wore an Afro.

The police got their big break in the case when they found the murder weapon. It, along with the gold ring stolen from Liuzza, was in the possession of a young black drug dealer named John Thompson.

John claimed he'd received the .357 Magnum and the ring in exchange for clickums—marijuana joints laced with PCP. Witnesses at his trial would later acknowledge that "hot" merchandise was often traded for drugs in the New Orleans underworld. But it looked bad for John, and it was about to get worse.

Shortly after the police arrested John for the murder of Ray Liuzza, they charged him with another crime: armed robbery. Witnesses had come forward to implicate John in a previously unsolved carjacking.

Robbery cases proceed faster than trials for

capital murder, and the prosecution moved especially fast on John's. They had his murder trial postponed while the robbery trial proceeded, and by the time John was ready to stand trial on charges for the Liuzza shooting, he had an armed robbery conviction under his belt.

Another man arrested in the murder case, Kevin Freeman, had been released for lack of evidence.

The robbery conviction made John's lawyer nervous, and he decided that it was a bad idea to put John on the stand in his own defense at the murder trial. Because of this, the jury never heard John tell the jury what he'd been telling his own lawyer: that he was innocent of *both* the robbery and the murder.

The robbery conviction hurt John in another way, too: prosecutor Gerry Deegan urged the court to consider the previous conviction as a reason to impose the death penalty.

At age 22, John was sentenced to death. He would serve most of his sentence at Louisiana's

Angola prison.

The Louisiana Crisis Assistance Center was working hard to find a lawyer to handle his appeals. In 1988, they succeeded: Michael L. Banks and Gordon Cooney Jr.—two lawyers with Philadelphia's Morgan Lewis—agreed to take John's case *pro bono* (at no charge).

Banks and Cooney are not criminal law specialists; their practices include mostly employment law and commercial litigation, respectively. But they were keen to take on a case that would make a difference on a personal level, and John Thompson's plight struck a chord.

It was rough going. Despite hard work by Banks and Cooney, eight execution dates were set for their client over the next 11 years. Banks and Cooney were desperate to find evidence that would exonerate their client. They hired a private investigator (PI) to work the front lines in New Orleans.

Just five weeks before John's May 20, 1999, date with the executioner, the PI presented

Banks and Cooney with a microfiche containing the results of a blood test.

The blood came from a pair of pants, and the pants came from a man named Stewart Lagarde. He was one of the victims in the carjacking that had led to John's armed robbery conviction. Lagarde had told police that during the carjacking, the attacker had been hurt, and had bled onto Lagarde's pants.

The pants were taken to a lab for processing back in 1985. The report of the results was dated April 9, 1985—two days before John's robbery trial began. The report showed that the attacker's blood was type B.

DISTRIBUTION OF BLOOD TYPES IN THE POPULATION	
Blood type	Percentage of total population (%)
O+	38.4
O–	7.7
A+	32.3
A–	6.5
B+	9.4
B–	1.7
AB+	3.2
AB–	0.7

However, John's blood type is type O.

On April 11, 1985, District Attorney Gerry Deegan had checked the evidence out of the police evidence room. The blood results, which would have excluded John as the perpetrator in the armed robbery, were never introduced at either the robbery trial or the murder trial.

Banks and Cooney moved quickly. Armed with the blood evidence, they advised District Attorney Harry Connick that they would be requesting a stay of execution for Thompson.

Connick didn't oppose the application; instead, he consented to it and launched an investigation into his office's role in the Thompson case.

On June 29, 1999, the court vacated Thompson's robbery conviction and ordered a new trial. It was the first step on John's lengthy journey to freedom.

In 2001, trial judge Patrick Quinlan vacated Thompson's death sentence, holding that the prosecution had improperly relied on the robbery conviction to convince the jury to choose capital punishment for John.

In 2002, the Fourth Circuit Court of Appeal

overturned John's murder conviction completely, ruling that "the State's intentional hiding of
exculpatory evidence in the armed robbery case
… led to [Thompson's] improper conviction in
that case and his subsequent decision not to
testify in the [murder] case because of the improper conviction." The court set a new trial.

At this trial, Banks and Cooney introduced
three new witnesses. One was Sheri Hartman
Kelly, who insisted that John was not the man
she'd seen shoot Ray Liuzza. The other two witnesses implicated Kevin Freeman, the man
who'd been arrested at the same time as John
Thompson. However, Freeman was already
dead: police had shot him while he was allegedly trying to break into cars some years later.

But the most important witness at the
2003 trial was Thompson himself, who finally
did what he had wanted to do 18 years earlier:
he took the stand in his own defense and pro-
claimed his innocence. It took less than an hour
for the jury to agree, and he was acquitted on

May 8. One day later, he walked out of prison a free man.

* * *

In September 2005, when Hurricane Katrina roared through New Orleans, the Thompsons' new house met the same fate as others in the low-lying black neighborhoods: it was flooded. The couple was forced to flee with family members to northwest Louisiana. In a letter appealing for financial help for his former client, lawyer Michael Banks asked: "I only hope that we can give him some of the tools that he so desperately needs to return his life to some semblance of normalcy."

Without Banks—and without Gordon Cooney, or the private detective who found the microfiche, or the rest of the community members who believed in him—John Thompson would not have a life to return to at all.

CHAPTER 2

The Death Penalty Today

According to the Death Penalty Information Center (DPIC) located in Washington, D.C., the death sentence is an available sentence in 40 U.S. states, as well as federally and in the U.S. military. In some states, such as New Hampshire, there have been no executions in almost three decades; in others, typically southern states, such as Texas, Alabama, and Florida, there are executions every year. In 2004,

23 prisoners were executed in Texas alone, out of a national total of 59.

In many states, although the death penalty remains on the books, it is rarely put into practice. As a matter of policy or practice in those states, death sentences are either not imposed or not carried out.

For example, while New York and Kansas have not formally abolished the death penalty as of the time this book was published, the death penalty was ruled unconstitutional in those states in 2004. The New York ruling was based on a defect in the instruction that judges gave to juries in that state. Juries were told that once a defendant was found guilty of a capital crime, they had to make a unanimous choice between the death penalty and life in prison. If they couldn't decide, the court would impose a sentence of 20–25 years with parole eligibility. The court found that this instruction was unconstitutional because it encouraged juries to impose a death sentence on defendants who didn't necessarily deserve it, in order to reach unanimity and avoid allowing the court to impose a sentence that permitted parole.

In Illinois, when the number of exonerations outpaced the number of executions in the late 1990s, Governor George Ryan declared a state moratorium on the death penalty in 2000. There have been no executions in Illinois since then, and several amendments to the death penalty laws have been made to respond to the issues raised. Maryland imposed its own moratorium, while awaiting the results of a study of racial bias in the application of the death penalty.

Another trend in death penalty policy in recent years has been for states to formally prohibit the imposition of the death penalty on convicts who suffer from cognitive impairment, described in some states as mental retardation.

The death penalty is not available in Canada, where it was abolished in 1976, or in Australia or most European countries. Fewer than half of the countries in the world retain the death penalty. In 2004, the United States was fourth on the list of countries with the most executions with 59; China led with at least 3,400, Iran followed with 159, and Vietnam was third with 64.

The number of executions in the United States peaked in 1999, when 98 people were executed. As the following chart demonstrates, the number of executions per year in the United States has climbed steadily in the last quarter of the 20th century.

A country or state's choice to retain the death penalty—or to carry it out when it's available—is very much a matter of philosophy. In some countries, the death penalty has religious roots. In the United States, the most common reasons death penalty supporters give for believing in the death penalty are deterrence and retributive justice.

Those who support the death penalty as a deterrent believe that the availability of the death penalty for certain crimes will discourage would-be offenders from committing those

U.S. EXECUTIONS

YEAR	NUMBER OF EXECUTIONS	YEAR	NUMBER OF EXECUTIONS
1989	16	1989	16
1991	14	1991	14
1993	38	1993	38
1995	56	1995	56
1997	74	1997	74
1999	98	1999	98

INTERNATIONAL STATISTICS

Ranking of top 10 countries internationally
in terms of rate of executions in 2004

China	>3400
Iran	159
Vietnam	64
United States	59
Saudi Arabia	33
Pakistan	15
Kuwait	9
Bangladesh	7
Egypt	6
Singapore	6

Source: Death Penalty Information Center

crimes. Most criminal sentences are designed with deterrence in mind (other sentencing objectives include rehabilitation and the protection of society).

It's difficult to measure the actual deterrent effect of a punishment, because an accurate measure would depend on our ability to determine how many crimes were *not* committed because the death penalty was available in the would-be criminal's jurisdiction. However, criminologists have sometimes drawn conclusions about deterrence by comparing the murder rate in abolitionist states (states without the death penalty) to the murder rate in retentionist states (states that have retained the death penalty). In the United States, these comparisons tend to suggest that the death penalty is not an especially reliable deterrent. For example, in abolitionist Maine, the murder rate per 100,000 people in 2004 was 1.2; in neighboring New Hampshire, which is retentionist, the murder rate in the same year was 1.4.

Retributive justice, which might be described as a reasoned form of revenge, is the second major argument in favor of the death penalty. Studies of jurors and of the general public suggest that those who strongly support the death penalty believe in retributive justice. Many people believe that certain criminals—especially those whose crimes are very repugnant—deserve to die for what they did. The idea of retributive justice sometimes has strong religious roots, although not all religious leaders support capital punishment (the Roman Catholic Church is a notable example of an abolitionist religious organization). However, many supporters of the death penalty come from a moral stance that has nothing to do with religion.

Most studies suggest that a modest majority of Americans favor the death penalty, even in many abolitionist states. In Canada, at the time of abolition in 1976, a *majority* of Canadians—between 55 and 75 percent—favored retaining capital punishment. Nevertheless, Canadian parliamentary representatives voted for abolition. Many of them decided that human rights issues were not an appropriate subject for political decision-making (borne out by a vote-by-vote survey of constituents).

In the United States, the loyalty of local politicians to the views of their constituents, most of whom truly believe in retributive justice, strongly influences retention of the death penalty in 40 states.

Retentionist states, along with U.S. politicians in general, have faced strong criticism in the international community for their views on capital punishment. According to Mary Robinson, the Human Rights Commissioner for the United Nations, "The increasing use of the death penalty in the United States and in a number of other states is a matter of serious concern and runs counter to the international community's expressed desire for the abolition of the death penalty."

Lethal injection is the most common method for carrying out executions in the United

States. All of the methods listed in the sidebar are still available in the United States, although the use of the first three is limited. In all retentionist states except Nebraska, lethal injection is a choice among several methods. (In Nebraska, electrocution is the only method of execution.)

> **EXECUTION METHODS IN THE UNITED STATES FROM 1977 TO 2004**
>
> - 2 prisoners were executed by firing squad
> - 3 prisoners were executed by hanging
> - 11 prisoners were executed by lethal gas (gas chamber)
> - 152 prisoners were executed by electrocution (electric chair)
> - 818 prisoners were executed by lethal injection

Firing Squad

Execution by firing squad was historically popular with the military in various countries. Inexpensive and involving little advance preparation and no specialized equipment, it could be performed almost anywhere and any time. In modern-day United States, only three states (Idaho, Oklahoma, and Utah) authorize executions by firing squad. In Idaho, firing squad is offered as a choice, with lethal injection also available. In Oklahoma, firing squad will only be used if both lethal injection and electrocution are ruled unconstitutional. In Utah, execution by firing squad is only available for those prisoners currently on death row who chose this method of execution. A law has now been passed in that state banning the practice.

For a firing squad execution, the prisoner sits strapped to a chair, usually wearing a hood or blindfold, with an oval bulletproof shield behind him or her. Sandbags are placed around the chair to absorb the prisoner's blood. A doctor locates the prisoner's heart with a stethoscope and attaches a white cloth target to mark the spot.

Five shooters—in Utah, volunteer peace officers from the county in which the conviction was made—are given .30-calibre rifles loaded with single rounds (sometimes one shooter is given a blank round). They shoot from 20 feet (6 m) away. The prisoner generally dies from blood loss as a result of rupture of the heart, the lungs, or a major blood vessel.

Four convicts still on Utah's death row chose execution by firing squad when offered the option; they will be allowed to die by this method if they are executed.

Hanging

Hanging was the principal method of execution in the United States until the 1890s. It is now authorized as an execution method only in the states of Washington and New Hampshire. In New Hampshire, a prisoner can only be hanged if lethal injection cannot be given for some reason; in Washington, hanging is offered as an alternative to lethal injection.

The day before a hanging, the prisoner is weighed to gauge the appropriate length of rope. A rehearsal, using sandbags, is carried out. Timing is important because if the real prisoner drops too quickly, he could be decapitated; if he drops too slowly, the method could fail, or death could be excruciatingly slow.

The rope is boiled, stretched, and lubricated. The inmate, his hands and feet bound, is blindfolded and escorted onto a platform fitted with a trap door. The rope is placed around his neck with the knot behind his left ear. At the executioner's order, the trap door is released and the inmate drops.

Ideally, death occurs when the prisoner's neck is cleanly dislocated. In practice, hangings have often been imperfect: the inmate falls too slowly and is asphyxiated.

The most recent hanging in the United States was the execution of Billy Bailey in Delaware in 1996. Bailey was convicted of shooting an elderly couple and was hanged after he refused to elect lethal injection.

Lethal Gas

Death by lethal gas (gas chamber) was used to execute 11 prisoners in the United States between 1977 and 2004. Lethal gas is an option in Arizona, California, Maryland, and Missouri. In a fifth state—Wyoming—a prisoner can only be gassed if lethal injection is ruled unconstitutional. In Arizona and Maryland, only inmates sentenced before specific dates can choose lethal gas; the method has been banned for those sentenced after those dates (in 1992 and 1994, respectively). Execution by lethal gas is not currently practiced anywhere else in the world.

The gas chamber was invented as a "humane" execution method in 1924. The inmate, in some cases wearing only boxer shorts, is strapped to a chair or gurney in an airtight chamber and hooked up to a long-distance stethoscope that can be read from outside the room to pronounce death. A pail of sulfuric acid is placed under the chair, and on the order, the executioner presses a lever that causes sodium cyanide crystals to mix with the acid, producing a toxic gas.

The prisoner dies from hypoxia, which occurs when the brain is starved of oxygen.

The procedure is reportedly painful, and prisoners who hold their breath die more slowly than those who take deep breaths, as instructed. The procedure was characterized as "cruel and unusual punishment" by a California court. When the ruling was upheld in circuit court in 1996, Judge Harry Pregerson wrote: "The district court's findings of extreme pain, the length of time this extreme pain lasts, and the substantial risk that inmates will suffer this extreme pain for several minutes require the conclusion that execution by lethal gas is cruel and unusual."

The most recent inmate to die in the gas chamber was Walter LaGrand, who was executed in Arizona in March 1999. He took 18 minutes to die after the cyanide was released. LaGrand was a German national, though he lived most of his life in the United States. His brother Karl LaGrand was executed by lethal injection the week before. Perhaps the most famous female inmate to die in the gas chamber was Barbara Graham, who was executed in 1955. Rumors of her possible innocence (or partial innocence) of the crime were rife at the time.

Electrocution

Ten U.S. states offer execution by electrocution—the electric chair. In Nebraska, the electric chair is the only available option; in Illinois and Oklahoma, it's available only if lethal injection is ruled unconstitutional. In seven states (Alabama, Arkansas, Florida, Kentucky, South Carolina, Tennessee, and Virginia), it's an option from which inmates can choose. Lethal injection is also an option in all of these states.

The electric chair has become an iconic symbol of capital punishment. It was invented in 1890, amid a fierce battle between early electricity entrepreneurs Edison and Westinghouse over direct current (DC) versus alternating current (AC) electrical service. The first electric chair operated on AC, which was Westinghouse's invention. The chair was developed with government assistance (but not Westinghouse's support), as a method to guarantee a swifter, less painful death than hanging or shooting.

The chair's first victim was William Kemmler, who was executed in 1890. (George Westinghouse was so concerned about the potential for bad press flowing from the use of his invention for this purpose that he contributed an enormous sum of money towards the prisoner's legal appeals, without success.) The first application of electricity failed to kill Kemmler, and the executioner was forced to run it a second time. When asked to comment on the execution, Westinghouse reportedly said, "They would have done better with an axe."

Modern-day electrocution executions require that the victim be shaved and strapped to a chair, with stiff belts across the body. Electrodes are placed on the prisoner's head and legs, to permit the electricity to pass through the body. From another room, the executioner sends 500–2000 volts through the body for about 30 seconds; the procedure is then repeated if the first attempt was not sufficient. The shock is often enough to cause the body to convulse violently, sometimes breaking or dislocating limbs, or causing the prisoner's eyeballs to pop out. The prisoner defecates and sometimes vomits blood, smoke and steam rise from the body, and there is a smell of burning. On autopsy, typically the victim's brain appears to be cooked.

These are "typical" events; botched electrocutions are even more horrific. Often, there is a long pause between the first and second applications of electricity while physicians try to determine whether the victim has died. In other cases, the victim's body catches fire and observers have seen flames. In the July 1999 execution of Allen Lee Davis, blood poured from the prisoner's mouth, forming a stain on his white shirt the size of a dinner plate. Justice Leander Shaw, who later heard a case on the constitutionality of electrocution, said "the color photos of Davis depict a man who—for all appearances—was brutally tortured to death by the citizens of

Florida." Nevertheless, the procedure was not ruled unconstitutional, and Florida still has the electric chair.

Lethal Injection

Lethal injection is by far the most common method of execution today. Since 1977, when Oklahoma first authorized the use of this method, 818 prisoners in the United States have been executed in this manner. All of the 40 retentionist states, except Nebraska, offer this method.

A prisoner about to be executed by lethal injection is strapped to a gurney or a fixed reclining table. Doctors cannot perform the procedure, because it is contrary to the principles of medical ethics (and the Hippocratic oath) to cause death. Specially trained attendants insert a substantial-gauge catheter into the prisoner's arm. (This is not always a simple procedure, especially if the prisoner has a history of using drugs by injection. For this reason, some states have an alternative available, such as electrocution.) A second catheter is inserted in the other arm, as a backup.

After the prisoner receives the drug Heparin—a blood thinner—a saline drip is begun. Then, the prisoner is either wheeled into the execution room, or the curtain is opened to allow witnesses to watch.

On the order, the executioner(s) adds three different chemicals, in succession, to the IV. First, the prisoner receives sodium thiopental, an anesthetic that typically causes unconsciousness in under a minute. The line is flushed and then pancuronium bromide, a powerful muscle relaxant, is added to stop the prisoner's breathing. The line is cleared again, and potassium chloride is added to stop the prisoner's heart. The injections take about three to five minutes to complete, and the prisoner is typically dead within eight minutes.

Despite the attention given to eliminate the prisoner's pain and suffering, the procedure has sometimes been botched. Examples have included struggles to insert the catheter (in one case, the prisoner was forced to help the executioner locate a usable vein), allergic reactions to the chemicals, clogged catheters, and improperly placed needles (into muscle instead of a vein—a very painful mistake). A clogged catheter plagued the 1994 execution of notorious John Wayne Gacy. A year later, Emmitt Foster took 30 minutes to die after too-tight restraints prevented the chemicals from circulating in his body and left him gasping and convulsing.

In recent years, some have raised concerns about the effects of the second drug—pancuronium bromide—that is used in lethal injection executions. Critics speculate that, since the drug is a muscle relaxant, it causes the prisoner to be completely still and might mask symptoms of pain that would be associated with its own effects and those of the potassium chloride. (The drug has been banned from veterinary practice because it masks the signs that anesthesia has not worked.) A University of Miami study of the autopsies of executed prisoners has suggested that 21 of the prisoners were likely conscious (even if immobile) at the time the potassium chloride began flowing, which means that they may have suffered considerably, though it was not apparent to witnesses.

Life on Death Row

While death by capital punishment can be painful and gruesome, life on death row is an intense waiting game. Death-row inmates are housed in maximum-security institutions, and typically spend nearly all of their time locked in their cells.

In an open letter describing his experiences on death row, John Thompson explained that for the first two years of his incarceration, he was allowed to see his sons only at Christmas. He writes of his parish prison: "There were 55 inmates housed on that tier, and 20 of them were being used as sex toys. This was my first time doing time, and although I had heard the stories and seen the movies, nothing compared to reality."

After leaving his parish prison, he was transferred to Angola prison, known by inmates as "the Farm" because there is a working farm on the 18,000-acre grounds. The prison was built on the location of a former plantation, and named after the African nation from which many of its slaves originated. Critics of the prison have suggested that the inmates' lives simply mirror those of the slaves who used to work the same land. Thompson didn't get to work on the farm—he spent much of his time in isolation, allowed out of his cell for only three hours of exercise per week. In some ways, the dreary isolation of death row was a blessing—Angola had a reputation as the "bloodiest prison in the South" due to a high number of inmate assaults. Thompson himself, in the years before he was isolated, lived in fear for his safety.

Thompson also reported feelings of extreme hopelessness and gloom, and a sense that death was very near.

The psychological trauma of isolation, and living under the threat of death are responsible, say some experts, for what has been called "death row syndrome," which can include delusional or suicidal thoughts.

In 1989, the United States sought to extradite Jens Soering, a German citizen charged with capital murders that took place in Virginia in 1985. He had fled to the United Kingdom. At his hearings before the European Court of Human Rights, Soering cited evidence of death row syndrome and argued that the conditions he would have to face on U.S. death row would be equivalent to

DEATH ROW SYNDROME

Death row syndrome (or death row phenomenon) is a legal (not medical) term used to describe a state of mental incapacity associated with life on death row. The peculiar characteristics of a death sentence—which include extended periods of isolation, the unrelenting threat of death, and uncertainty about the timing of execution—have been found to produce a cluster of symptoms in some prisoners. This cluster includes delusions, suicidal tendencies, and the loss of the will to live.

torture. The international court agreed, and Soering was extradited only after prosecutors agreed
not to seek the death penalty in his case.

In fact, life on death row can be so trau-
matic that some experts believe the experience can lead certain inmates to abandon their
rights to further appeals and volunteer for the
death penalty. This argument was raised in the
defense of Connecticut inmate Michael Ross,
who attempted suicide three times in his 17
years on death row, where he was isolated for
23 hours a day. Ross's lawyers sought to prevent
his 2005 execution on the basis that he was not
mentally competent to do what he purported to
do: volunteer for execution. Death-row expert
Dr. Stuart Grassian contributed the following
opinion to the lawyers' brief: "The conditions
of confinement are so oppressive, the helpless-
ness endured in the roller coaster of hope and
despair so wrenching and exhausting, that ultimately the inmate can no longer bear it, and
then it is only in dropping his appeals that he

has any sense of control over his fate."

An important contributor to psychological disturbance on the part of death-row inmates is the time interval between sentencing and execution. The average time on death row for inmates executed in 2000 was just short of 12 years, with some inmates waiting over 20 years. Concerns have been raised that these long wait times amount to a second sentence, so that the inmate gets not only death, but also a decade of near-solitary confinement.

Of course, an inmate's waiting time is often extended because of legal issues. Some inmates pursue appeals to secure their freedom; seek new trials to prove their innocence; or bring constitutional challenges to various aspects of the death penalty or the laws or law enforcement practices used to convict them. In his 2000 report, "A Broken System: Error Rates in Capital Cases, 1973–1995," James Liebman notes, "Capital sentences do spend a long time under judicial review. As this study documents, how-

ever, judicial review takes so long precisely because American capital sentences are so persis-
tently and systematically fraught with error that
seriously undermines their reliability."

Inmates can leave death row for reasons
other than having been exonerated as innocent
of their crimes. Sometimes an inmate wins an
appeal of his/her criminal conviction or his/her
sentence. Inmates can also be granted clemency and have their sentences reduced (to life
imprisonment, for example) on compassionate
grounds.

Since 1979, 229 prisoners have been moved
off death row on compassionate grounds. In
some cases, politicians will commute the sentences of all inmates on death row, or all those
placed on death row during their term of office.
The most recent example of this was Governor
George Ryan's 2003 grant of clemency to all
death-row inmates in Illinois, which came in
the wake of serious allegations of corruption in
the Illinois justice system.

Clemency can also be granted case by case. Reasons cited for doing this include doubts about the inmate's guilt, a sense that the death penalty is disproportionate to the crime, remorse and/or religious conversion on the part of the inmate, pleas for clemency by the victim's family, factors relating to the inmate's cognitive abilities or mental health, concerns about racial bias in sentencing, unwillingness to execute an inmate who was a juvenile at the time of the crime, and the anti-capital punishment stance of the politician granting clemency. According to the Death Penalty Information Center (an anti-capital punishment organization), of the 229 prisoners granted clemency since 1979, at least 20 were based on doubts about the inmate's guilt.

The NAACP keeps quarterly statistics on the death-row population. As of July 1, 2005, there were 3,415 people on death row throughout the United States. (This number is down slightly from the 2002 figure of 3,697.) Only 54 women (or less than two percent of the total) are currently on death row. Less than one percent of the total are juveniles; a U.S. Supreme Court ruling in March 2005 found it unconstitutional to execute a person whose crime was committed before the age of 18. The average age of inmates at execution varies from 39 to 44 years; overall, due to long wait times, the death-row population is aging, with some inmates in their 70s and 80s.

The NAACP reports that overall, the number of white inmates (about 45.5 percent) exceeds that of black inmates (about 42 percent) in U.S. prisons. In some states, however, the percentage of black inmates on death row is significantly higher, for example 69 percent in Texas and 70 percent in Pennsylvania.

Concerns about racial bias in convictions and sentencing have long plagued the U.S. justice system, and a few states are currently studying the issue. Black accused who kill white victims have been disproportionately more likely to be sentenced to death than accused who kill victims of the same race. A recent Philadelphia study found that African Americans accused of murder, such as Larry Griffin and John Thompson, were almost four times more likely to be sentenced to death than accused of other racial backgrounds who had committed similar crimes.

The application of the death penalty is even more clearly biased against the poor. Horror stories abound about accused who received the penalty after being represented by incompetent lawyers. According to Amnesty International USA, 95 percent of people sentenced to death cannot afford their own attorneys.

CHAPTER 3

How Innocent People End Up on Death Row

Most of the men and women on death row in the United States are guilty of horrible crimes. In his book *The Death Penalty on Trial: Crisis in American Justice,* Bill Kurtis describes some of the Illinois death-row inmates whose sentences Governor George Ryan commuted to life in prison in January 2003: "Jacqueline Williams cut the full-term fetus from the belly of the pregnant woman she and Fedell

Caffey had killed because she wanted a baby. Although the baby lived and was kidnapped, the two other children of the victim were killed. Daniel Edwards lured Steve Small, the publisher of the *Kankakee Journal* newspaper, to the garage of a home he was renovating, stuffed him in the trunk of a car, and then buried him alive."

Many of the men and women on death row may not support capital punishment, however, they accept that they are awaiting execution because capital punishment is part of the justice system in their state, that they have committed acts defined as capital crimes, and that a jury of their peers has convicted them of those acts.

According to the Death Penalty Information Center, of the 986 applications of the death penalty in the United States between 1977 and October 6, 2005, 117 prisoners actually volunteered for execution. Notable on this list were Aileen Wournos, the prostitute turned vigilante, whose story was the subject of a feature film entitled *Monster;* and Timothy McVeigh, the primary perpetrator of the 1995 Oklahoma City bombing that killed dozens of people. While McVeigh gave no final statement at the time of his execution, he did deliver a poem by British poet William Ernest Henley to his prison warden. Entitled "Invictus" (or "unconquerable"), its final lines read:

> *Beyond this place of wrath and tears*
> *Looms but the horror of the shade,*
> *And yet the menace of the years*
> *Finds, and shall find me, unafraid.*
> *It matters not how strait the gate,*
> *How charged with punishments the scroll,*
> *I am the master of my fate:*
> *I am the captain of my soul.*

But not all death-row inmates approach their fate with such stoic resignation—and with good reason. According to a study of judicial error completed in 2000, Columbia School of Law professor James Liebman writes: "[O]ur 23 years' worth of results reveal a death penalty system collapsing under the weight of its own mistakes." He explains that a review of capital cases from 1973 to 1995 reveals "serious, reversible error" in 68 percent of the cases. The U.S. Senate Committee on the Judiciary, not a partisan campaign for an anti-death penalty platform, commissioned Liebman's study.

A suspect's journey from investigation to sentence is lengthy and complicated, along which police officers, lawyers, jurors, and judges examine the suspect's case. Myriad small, individual decisions determine the course of the investigation, the prosecution, and if the suspect is convicted, the sentencing process.

Errors and omissions can occur at any stage, as can corruption. While any individual error or bad faith action might seem minor at the time, some decisions can create a cascade effect, influencing other decisions, ultimately the result of the trial, and the decision to sentence an accused to die for his alleged crime.

Investigation

The first stage at which mistakes can happen—
the crime investigation—mostly involves the
narrowing down of a broad spectrum of possi-
bilities into a single theory about how the crime
was committed. Bill Kurtis notes "[p]erhaps the
most common fault with criminal investigations is their failure to explore all the possible
suspects. When attention begins to focus on a
single individual, too often the detectives are
called off the general hunt to go after the single
target. Tunnel vision sets in."

This tunnel vision can lead to the abandon-
ment of lines of deductive reasoning that point
the finger of guilt at a totally different suspect.
In a prominent New York City case, five youths
were convicted of a Central Park rape, based on
their confessions. It was later determined that
the boys' confessions were coerced; instead, a
single adult perpetrator was responsible for the
crime that sent five young men to jail.

Investigative tunnel vision also appears to

have been at the root of the 1974 death-row sentences handed down to four New Mexico men implicated in a kidnapping, rape, and murder. Ronald Keine, one of the four men, appeared on the Larry King Live show in late 2004 to discuss the case. At the time of the murder, Keine had been a member of what he called "a drinking club with a motorcycle problem," and he and three associates had driven through New Mexico the week *after* a young college student was brutally raped and murdered. The key witness in the case against Keine, Thomas Gladish, Richard Greer, and Clarence Smith was a woman who later admitted to having been coerced to testify against the bikers, after having been "handed around as a sex toy" by police detectives investigating the case.

An investigation by the *Detroit News* raised serious concerns about the conviction of the four men, whom police had originally picked up for punching a hitchhiker. Reporters proved the men had no connection with the murder. The subsequent re-investigation led to the exoneration of the four, who, at the time, were purportedly "10 days away from the gas chamber." The murder weapon was traced to another person, who admitted to the killing.

Trial

Even if an investigation isn't marred by corruption or incompetence, the trial offers more opportunities for error, this time on the part of the lawyers on either side. Says Kurtis: "[S]ubjective choices and decisions ... [for example, choosing one expert to testify over another when their opinions conflict] happen in one form or another many times in every trial. Most have no bearing on the verdict; they are the mysterious "technicalities" we hear so much about. But some, whether they are innocent, absent-minded moments of forgetfulness or intentional acts of hiding evidence from the other side, can have life-or-death consequences."

In his book, Kurtis studied the exoneration

of Ray Krone, who was put on Arizona's death row for the murder of a bartender with whom he had been on a couple of dates. Krone was known as the "snaggletooth killer" because his conviction relied heavily on a finding that his crooked teeth matched the post-mortem (inflicted after death) bite marks found around the victim's nipple.

The prosecutor, relying on the evidence of State Senator and bite-mark specialist Dr. Raymond Rawson, produced a videotape to demonstrate to the jury that Krone's teeth matched the victim's bite mark. Not only did this conclusion seal Krone's fate, but also the post-mortem bite, with its necrophiliac implications, amounted to an aggravating factor that supported the death sentence for Krone.

A later review—prompted by interest in the case from Krone's cousin—revealed that either an investigator or the prosecution itself had concealed that another prominent bite-mark specialist, Dr. Sperber (who was the mentor of the investigator who created the cast against which Krone's teeth were compared), had told the investigator that the mark was *not* consistent with Krone's teeth. Dr. Sperber's opinion had prompted the investigator (or the prosecution, if they knew) to search for a more favorable specialist. However, prosecutors are required, under the rules of discovery, to disclose to the defense the opinions of *all* specialists consulted in a criminal case. That didn't happen, and Krone, a former serviceman with no prior criminal record, was sent to death row.

But it wasn't the bite-mark error that ultimately exonerated Krone after 10 years in prison; it was a *separate* error. After a second jury found him guilty again, his lawyers obtained a court order for DNA testing. Tests of saliva on victim Kim Ancona's tank top linked another man to the crime. Kenneth Phillips was a paroled sex offender living a few hundred yards from the bar. A month after Ancona's murder, while the wrong man languished in jail, Phillips was arrested for another sexual assault and DNA samples were taken. The odds that the saliva on Kim Ancona's clothing was *not* Phillips's were 1.3 *quadrillion* to one.

Apart from the bite mark, which was characterized as scientific evidence, all of the other evidence against Krone was circumstantial. Bill Kurtis believes that "… death penalty cases should not hinge on circumstantial evidence. There is too high a risk that the wrong version of events will be sold [to the jury] by a persuasive prosecutor."

If Kim Ancona had been murdered a couple of decades earlier, Ray Krone would almost certainly have been executed. DNA evidence is a fairly new tool in criminal investigations, and the first exoneration of a death-row inmate based on DNA evidence did not come until 1993, the year after Krone was first convicted.

Missing the saliva evidence in the Krone case was a fairly subtle mistake. In "A Broken System," James Liebman's study maintains that subtlety of judicial errors is often responsible for putting innocent people on death row. According to Liebman, on average, it took three separate "judicial inspections" (appeals, or judicial review applications) to uncover the errors he cites in the 68 percent of fully reviewed capital cases. But, as previously mentioned, the overwhelming majority of accused people sentenced to death row cannot afford private legal representation.

When an accused cannot afford to choose and hire his own lawyer, the state is required to provide one. The quality of legal services provided by overburdened duty counsel and state-sponsored lawyers is highly variable, and all too often miserably inadequate. The Liebman report places the incompetence of attorneys (including prosecutors) at the top of the list of causes of errors in capital cases.

Examples of the incompetence of counsel representing those facing death row abound. In their book *Legal Lynching: The Death Penalty and America's Future*, authors Rev. Jesse L. Jackson Sr., Jesse L. Jackson Jr., and Bruce Shapiro note that in recent years, the Texas Court of Appeals has declined to consider three petitions from death-row prisoners whose lawyers spent important parts of the inmates' trials sleeping.

Nine years after Benjamin Harris was sentenced to death row for murder, a Washington district judge overturned Harris's conviction, based on the incompetence of his lawyer. The lawyer spent only two hours reviewing the case with his client, and interviewed 3 out of 32 available witnesses. Unfortunately, instead of providing Harris with a retrial, the prosecution opted instead to have him declared insane and confined to a mental hospital.

When Oklahoma's Ronald Keith Williamson was tried for capital murder in 1988, his state-sponsored lawyer was paid only $3,200 to mount a defense. In contrast, some expert witnesses in today's high profile cases charge 10 times that much for a mere appearance. The lawyer failed to uncover and present evidence that another man had actually confessed to the murder. Williamson was convicted and spent more than 10 years on death row.

Ernest Ray Willis was convicted in 1987 of the death of two women in a house fire. At the time of trial, Willis was dazed from antipsychotic medication that his jailers had inappropriately administered. The prosecution capitalized on the medication side effects and portrayed him as cold-hearted and satanic. His own lawyers were ineffective and underprepared, having spent only three hours with their client. Willis, who had no prior criminal record, was sentenced to death row.

Seventeen years later, when the investigation was re-opened, investigators discovered that there was no evidence of arson associated with the house fire; instead, it appeared to have been caused by faulty wiring. The prosecutor who re-opened the case said of Willis's exoneration: "[Willis] simply did not do the crime … I'm sorry this man was on death row for so long and that there were so many lost years." Willis was released with $100 and the clothes on his back.

Supreme Court Justice Ruth Bader Ginsburg once said the following about lawyers in capital cases: "I have yet to see a death penalty case among the dozens coming to the Supreme Court on eve-of-execution stay applications in which the defendant was well represented ... People who are well-represented at trial do not get the death penalty." Journalist turned death-row prisoner and political activist Mumia Abu-Jamal expressed this sentiment more succinctly: "Them's that got the capital don't get the punishment."

The rate of exonerations of previously convicted inmates has risen dramatically since the mid-'70s. One 2005 study by Samuel R. Gross (the lawyer who prepared the report that led to the re-opening of the Larry Griffin case) and colleagues studied all exonerations (not only death-row cases) between 1989 and 2003. The study stated:

This rapid increase in reported exonerations probably reflects the combined effects of three interrelated trends. First, the growing availability and sophistication of DNA identification technology. … Second, the singular importance of the DNA revolution has made exonerations increasingly newsworthy. … And third, this increase in attention has in turn led to a substantial increase in the number of false convictions that in fact do come to light and end in exonerations, by DNA or other means. More resources are devoted to the problem—there are now, for example, forty-one Innocence Projects in thirty-one states—and judges, prosecutors, defense lawyers, and police officers have all become more aware of the danger of false convictions.

According to the study, the investigative and justice systems are more likely to make errors in capital murder cases than other cases. Gross speculates that this is partly due to the enormous pressure placed on prosecutors to quickly find and arrest a perpetrator for crimes that shock society. The death penalty is also a strong motive for the actual killer to frame somebody else for the crime. Says Gross: "We are most likely to convict innocent defendants in those cases in which their very lives are at stake."

The Gross study found that in 43 percent of cases of people exonerated for murder, the convicted person was intentionally misidentified, falsely accused, or framed by somebody else. In 15 percent of cases, the wrongfully convicted person had actually confessed to the crime, usually as a result of extreme pressure by police. Wrongful confessions are much more commonly made by juveniles, accused with cognitive deficits (who are mentally retarded), or mentally ill accused. Children between the ages of 12 and 15 who were later exonerated of their crimes gave false confessions a shocking 69 percent of the time.

MENTAL RETARDATION

"Mental retardation" as a legal concept generally refers narrowly to a situation in which a person's IQ falls well below the bottom of the average range. This definition differs from "mental disability"—the modern medical term used to describe a wide range of conditions that can affect intellectual function.

In the tragic "Ford Heights Four" case, 17-year-old Paula Gray, who was borderline mentally retarded, gave a false confession in 1978 that implicated four other defendants in a murder. All five (Gray and the four men) were convicted, and two of the men were sent to death row. All five have since been exonerated by DNA evidence, and the real killers have confessed to the crime.

The shocking trends uncovered by the Gross investigation led the authors to realize that the 340 exonerations they had documented were only the tip of the iceberg. They conclude "[a]ny plausible guess at the total number of miscarriages of justice in America in the last 15 years must be in the thousands, perhaps tens of thousands."

In summary, the opportunities for the machinery of justice to make a wrong turn that can lead to a wrongful conviction, or to keep an inmate on death row when he should be exonerated, appear at every stage of the path from investigation to sentencing. Potential errors include the following:

During the Investigation

- A suspect can be accidentally misidentified, and yet innocent witnesses can be so convinced of his involvement that it later takes DNA evidence to clear him.
- A suspect can be misidentified or implicated on purpose by jailhouse snitches, or by the real perpetrator, because these witnesses have strong motivations to lie.
- A suspect can be targeted far too early in the investigation process due to investigator "tunnel vision."

- A suspect can be targeted, despite doubt about his involvement, because prosecutors are under extreme pressure to make an arrest in a crime that shocks the community.
- Innocent errors can be made that may seem minor at the time, but which influence the outcome of the investigation and draw the focus away from the real perpetrator and onto an innocent person.
- Police pressure can induce suspects, especially young or cognitively impaired ones, to confess to a crime they did not commit.

At the Trial

- People accused of capital crimes are statistically less likely to be able to afford private lawyers; the accused are usually forced to rely on public defenders of variable quality.
- The average competence of lawyers who represent people accused of capital crimes has proven to be unacceptably low.
- Capital cases are often assigned to the most

experienced prosecutors, whose experience usually far exceeds that of the defendant's lawyer. This fact makes the trial odds unequal regardless of the facts.

- There is extra pressure on prosecutors to secure convictions in the cases that attract capital punishment; this can motivate prosecutors to pursue "wins" rather than true justice.
- Cases built on circumstantial evidence are dangerously speculative, especially when the defendant's life is at stake.
- The use of jailhouse snitches and informants is especially problematic in capital cases (the snitches are sometimes suspects themselves and are highly motivated to lie or place the blame on someone else.)

After the Trial
- Appeal courts are much more inclined to defer to, rather than overturn, the decision of a lower court.
- Errors in the factual record become entrenched

as an accepted part of "the story" and are increasingly difficult to challenge the more time that elapses after the original investigation.

• The conditions under which inmates live can generate apathy and false resignation and can lead even innocent convicts to abandon their legal rights to pursue exoneration.

Of course, it's impossible to determine how many innocent people have been sent to death row in the United States, or how many have actually been executed. The Gross study puts the figure of death-row prisoners *actually exonerated* at 75 between 1989 and 2003. The Death Penalty Information Center lists 122 exonerations between 1973 and the present (the most recent being in November 2005).

There is no documented case of a person being exonerated *after* having been put to death; however, rumors of an executed person's innocence have persisted in a number of cases. An organization called Equal Justice USA (EJU-SA) investigated the issue of innocents actually executed, and their work yielded 16 case histories in which there were objectively significant doubts about the guilt of the accused. Larry Griffin made the EJUSA list.

So did Gary Graham, who was executed by lethal injection in Texas in June 2000. Graham had been convicted of murder based primarily on the testimony of a single eyewitness. Two other witnesses disagreed that Graham was the perpetrator. After Graham was convicted, three jurors from his case petitioned unsuccessfully for his exoneration after learning about the contradictory witness evidence.

If we accept the inferences drawn by many of the researchers who have studied the incidence of judicial error, we must conclude that there are people in the United States who have been investigated, tried, convicted, sentenced, and executed while completely innocent of the crimes with which they were charged. The next three chapters present the stories of some of the luckier ones.

CHAPTER 4

DNA as a Key to Innocence

Deoxyribonucleic acid (DNA) contains the unique genetic code that defines an individual's biological development. The most famous application of the discovery of DNA is in the field of forensics. Scientists can now use the information in tiny quantities of human fluids or tissues—blood, saliva, semen, hair, skin—to establish which person has left behind a trace of his or her presence on other people, or on objects in the environment.

In criminal justice terms, DNA can implicate a guilty person or exonerate an innocent one.

The first time DNA science was used in the United States to exonerate an innocent convict was in 1989, when the Cook County Circuit Court in Illinois vacated Gary Dotson's conviction for a rape that had occurred 10 years earlier. From that date onward, DNA evidence has played a role in one-third to one-half of all exonerations.

While DNA test results were a secondary factor in a few earlier cases, the first person to walk off death row as a direct result of DNA testing was Oklahoma's Robert Lee Miller Jr.

Miller was a young black man living in a neighborhood near the scene of the 1986 rape and murder of an 83-year-old woman. Police investigating the crime knew that a young black man who was a type A secretor—a blood type shared by 25 percent of the population—had killed the woman. After going door to door, police built a list of 23 suspects who fit the profile. One of them was Miller.

Robert Miller was an unusual young man. Somewhat mentally unstable, he believed he had special powers, and he was deeply religious. When police interviewed him, he told them he could "see through the eyes of the killer." Demonstrating this, and with the help of details fed to him by police, he described three crimes for which he had become a suspect. Unfortunately, his vision through criminal eyes was hardly 20/20: besides other key inconsistencies, he described the age of the first rape-and-murder victim as just a few years older than himself. But he was 27, and the victim was 83.

During the interview, Miller denied more than 70 times his own involvement in the crimes.

Nevertheless, the prosecution characterized the videotaped statements as an admission of guilt, and Miller was eventually convicted and sentenced to death. In early 1988, the use of DNA evidence in criminal trials was in its infancy. At Miller's trial, a couple of experts testified about samples of blood, semen, and hair. Describing the basic (non-DNA) biological characteristics of these, the experts established that some evidence was consistent with Miller, or at least a man *like* him—black and type A. Some hairs couldn't be accounted for, but these were ignored. And there was a subtype difference between one of their samples and Miller's biology that was explained away by saying that the sample tested that way because it contained a mix of the killer's and the victim's fluids.

A few years later, DNA testing had come a long way. Between 1992 and 1996, the biological evidence collected in the Miller case was tested three times by different labs. In conducting the testing, scientists considered three possible perpetrators: Miller, a man named Ronald Lott, and another man named Roderick Wilson. Interpretation of DNA test results is complicated, but the results as reported by the scientific experts can be summarized as follows:

- 1992 tests, conducted by Serological Research Institute: Miller is excluded as the perpetrator.
- 1995 tests, conducted by LabCorp: any of Miller, Lott, or Wilson could be the killer.
- 1995 re-tests, conducted by LabCorp: Miller is not excluded as the perpetrator.
- 1996 re-tests, conducted by LabCorp: testing, focusing on semen in particular, excludes both Miller and Wilson as the possible provider of 100 percent of samples tested.

Despite being excluded by the very first round of tests, Miller continued to languish on death row. When he was retried based on the DNA evidence in 1997, prosecutors continued to argue for the validity of his "confession" and for his presence at the crime scene, despite what was widely accepted, by experts, as conclusive DNA evidence that Ronald Lott, not Miller, had committed the rapes.

Unlike the prosecutors, the jury was ready

to put their trust in science. At the retrial, they acquitted Miller.

Prosecutors scrambled, even in the face of scientific evidence of his innocence, to indict Robert Miller anew. They approached Ronald Lott in prison and told him that unless he agreed to implicate Miller, he (Lott) would be facing the death penalty based on the semen evidence. Lott rejected the deal that, he was told, would save his own life. Prosecutors dropped the charges, based on what they described not as innocence, but as a "lack of evidence."

But the era of DNA as a key to innocence had begun, and there would be no turning back. As Bill Kurtis wrote in *The Death Penalty on Trial: Crisis in American Justice,* "[t]he entry hole blown open by DNA would reveal a system awash in flaws, a system so institutionalized it had lost sight of the end goal, justice."

* * *

EXONERATION

The majority of commentators consider a person to have been exonerated if:
1. He/she is acquitted of the crime; or
2. His/her conviction is overturned, the prosecution elects not to lay new charges, and there is credible evidence to support actual, not just technical, innocence (i.e., that the person really didn't do the crime).

Since the Robert Lee Miller Jr. case, DNA has helped to free at least seven other innocent men on death row, and to exonerate an eighth, Frank Lee Smith.

Unfortunately for Smith, the good news came 10 months too late: after serving 14 years on Florida's death row, Smith died of cancer while awaiting execution for the 1985 murder of eight-year-old Shandra Whitehead.

Beginning in 1990, Smith's lawyers, believing in his innocence, had fought unsuccessfully for the right to have DNA testing done.

Despite the fact that the prosecution had biological evidence from the victim all along, the second half of the DNA equation—samples from Smith—were not collected or tested until *after* he died in prison. The posthumous samples showed conclusively that Smith did not kill Shandra Whitehead.

Smith's wrongful conviction, which formed the subject of a 2002 PBS episode of *Frontline* called "Requiem for Frank Lee Smith," was typical of wrongful convictions. Smith found his way to death row after being misidentified by witnesses who were anxious to help prosecutors put someone behind bars for a crime that had shocked the community.

Smith's life before death row was typical, too. He had grown up poor, and suffered from schizophrenia. Like many other prison long-timers, Shandra Whitehead's death wasn't the first crime that he'd had to answer for. The jury who sentenced him to death did so knowing that he had two previous convictions for manslaughter.

Still, he *didn't* commit the crime that sent him to death row.

Barry Scheck, the founder of the first Innocence Project, harshly criticized the justice system in Florida. Citing the state's abysmal record for wrongful convictions—Florida leads the way in death-row exonerations with 21 (out of a U.S. total of 122)—Scheck expressed dismay at the lack of reasonable access to post-conviction DNA testing for Florida inmates:

> *Starting October 1, 2002, all inmates in the Florida prison system who think they can prove their innocence with a post-conviction DNA test have two years to file some fairly complex motions seeking such relief. Very few of these inmates can afford a lawyer to file such a motion. They are not entitled to get a lawyer appointed until they file an appropriate motion. Yet our experience over the last decade at the Innocence Project teaches us that it takes, on the average, three or four years, with our help, to gather the necessary tran-*

*scripts, police reports, and lab reports
to file a sound post-conviction DNA
motion.*

Frank Lee Smith's motion for testing was denied because it was filed outside the two-year waiting period, and Scheck predicts that, in Florida, "dozens of inmates who could prove their innocence with a test will be unable to do so because of this unfair time limit."

* * *

In the scramble to lay the legal groundwork needed for post-conviction DNA tests, it helps to have a support network. Ryan Matthews, the most recent death-row exoneree to be freed by DNA evidence, was fortunate to be the son of a loving and determined mother. Ryan's mother, Pauline, was horrified to find her son on death row at age 18.

The crime that sent Ryan Matthews to death

row was the shooting of Tommy Vanhoose. Well liked in his community of Bridge City, near New Orleans, Louisiana, Vanhoose was the owner of Comeaux' Grocery Store on the bank of the Mississippi.

According to witnesses, a single masked gunman came into the store and demanded money. When Vanhoose resisted, the gunman shot him four times. Leaving Vanhoose alive but bleeding to death, the robber pulled off his ski mask and jumped through the window of a waiting getaway car.

Later that day, police stopped a car that matched the description of the getaway car. In fact, it *almost* matched—the passenger window on this car, the window through which the fleeing robber was supposed to have jumped, couldn't be opened, and had been that way as long as the driver, Travis Hayes, could remember.

The police arrested Ryan Matthews and Travis Hayes anyway. After six hours of interrogation, Hayes told police that he had driven the car to Comeaux' Grocery Store and had waited outside for Ryan. Fifteen minutes later, said Hayes, he heard shots, and Ryan came out.

Hayes's confession made it easier for investigators to ignore another important glitch in the evidence: witnesses to the robbery had described the robber as a small person, just 5'5" or 5'6" but Ryan is at least 6' tall.

It didn't matter. Ryan was indicted, and a jury was selected. Although the crime occurred in an area where racial minorities make up one-third of the population, 11 of the 12 jury members were white; only one was African-American, like Ryan.

The trial proceeded with unusual alacrity. On the second day of trial, the prosecution presented evidence until 10 at night. The defense moved to rest. But instead of adjourning until the next day, the judge ordered the prosecution and defense to make closing statements to an exhausted jury. At the end of those, in response to a second request from the defense to rest, the judge ordered the jury not home to bed, but to the jury room to begin its deliberations.

Sequestered in the jury room in the middle of the night, the 12 exhausted jurors couldn't agree on a verdict. At 4:20 a.m., they advised the judge of their hung status. The judge refused to accept the deadlock, and ordered them to resume deliberating. Just 45 minutes later, at 5 a.m., they returned a verdict of guilty.

Two days later, Ryan was sentenced to death for the murder of Tommy Vanhoose, and began his sojourn on Angola's death row.

Pauline Matthews worried about Ryan in jail. She couldn't touch her son when he was in Angola, and she'd learned that the guards had failed, on more than one occasion, to give Ryan the medicine he needed for the seizures he'd been prone to since childhood. The missed treatment has been blamed for permanent brain damage that Ryan apparently suffered while on death row. Brain damage was the last thing Ryan needed; intelligence tests conducted in preparation for trial (before the brain damage) had indicated that the teenager had serious problems with adaptation and intellectual functioning, and an IQ of just 71. The commonly accepted cutoff for mental retardation is 70.

Pauline helped bring Ryan's case to the attention of Billy Sothern and Clive Stafford Smith at the Louisiana Crisis Assistance Center. Sothern and Smith, in turn, sought the help of Barry Scheck and the Innocence Project at New York's Cardozo School of Law.

Ryan's legal team focused on two leads. One was based on allegations of improper treatment by the prosecution of an identification witness: one of the witnesses who'd said a small man

THE INNOCENCE PROJECT

The Innocence Project is dedicated to seeing the wrongfully convicted exonerated through post-conviction DNA testing. Since it began in 1992, the organization has helped exonerate more than 160 wrongfully convicted persons. Furthermore, hundreds of individuals each year are cleared before their cases go to trial. There are now Innocence Projects in at least 40 states and in 2 Canadian provinces.

had committed the crime. The second lead was a report that another prisoner, Rondell Love, had reportedly bragged to other inmates that he had murdered Vanhoose. Ryan's defense team obtained declarations from three people that they'd overheard Love's remarks.

Rondell Love had pled guilty to another murder near the scene of the Comeaux' Grocery Store shooting. The investigation of that murder had generated DNA evidence linking Love to the crime. Ryan Matthews' lawyers knew there was a source of DNA evidence in Ryan's case—the ski mask discarded by the killer in his haste to get away.

The lawyers negotiated access to the mask—an exhibit from the trial—and arranged for the DNA samples taken from it to be compared with Love's samples.

The results matched Love and excluded Ryan and his "accomplice," Travis Hayes.

Armed with the DNA evidence and the allegations that the prosecution had mistreated the identification witness, Ryan's lawyers began clamoring for his release in the spring of 2003.

Said Billy Sothern to the *New York Times* in July 2003: "[T]his is the trifecta in terms of what's wrong with the death penalty. Ryan was a juvenile at the time of the murder, he's retarded, and he's innocent."

In August, the defense team applied to have prosecutor David Wolff barred from representing the state in the hearing about the new evidence. Controversy had surrounded the prosecutor's performance at trial, and Pauline Matthews was reported as saying, "We can't trust the people who put Ryan on death row to let him go."

The application was unsuccessful, and Wolff continued to fight for Ryan's continued incarceration, contending, even in the face of the DNA evidence, that there was "absolutely no merit" to the defense's claim that Ryan was innocent. In his writings on the influence of confessions, Barry Scheck, an expert in wrongful convictions and a member of Ryan's defense team, attributed much of the prosecution's resistance to the fact that Travis Hayes had confessed. Scheck said that despite the growing proof that false confessions are commonplace, "it's always harder for prosecutors to accept" that a convict is innocent when he—or an accomplice—has confessed to the crime. But Scheck maintained a sense of hope: "[I]t's clear to me that the district attorney's office is coming to grips with the significance and implications of the DNA evidence, and they are bound to follow the leads."

Finally, in April 2004—a year after the conclusive DNA results were in—the state relented. Ryan would get his new trial.

Then, in a surprise move two months later, the state went one step further: they released Ryan on bail. He was released into his mother's care, to be kept under house arrest with the help of an electronic tracking anklet. Pauline Matthews was relieved; now that he was in her care, her son would be certain to get the medication he needed for his seizure disorder.

On August 9, 2004, prosecutors announced that there would be no new trial. Based on their review of the DNA evidence, they were dropping all charges against Ryan Matthews.

The 24-year-old was innocent. It had taken years, the help of cutting-edge science, and the dedicated efforts of a whole panel of lawyers; but another innocent man was off death row.

* * *

In arguing for early access to DNA testing, and for the need for prosecutors to consider that less scientific methods of finding the truth can sometimes be flawed, Peter Neufeld, co-founder of the first Innocence Project, has said: "What should govern … [access to testing applications] is not legal precedent, not factual loopholes, but the fundamental obligation of everyone in the criminal justice system to ensure that only the factually guilty suffer in prison."

CHAPTER 5

Cognitive Impairment

In recent years, two of the most troubling death-row issues to attract the attention of state and federal courts have been youth and cognitive impairment (mental retardation).

Studies about young accused strongly suggest that the practices of our justice system operate unfairly against suspects who were under the age of 18 when they committed their crimes. Young people who commit crimes tend to be motivated by different reasons than their adult counterparts. Some of these reasons relate to factors unique to adolescence: poor impulse control and the inability to predict consequences, for example. Also, the investigation and investigators easily influence and intimidate young accused, and in particular first-time offenders.

Until last summer, the United States was one of a very short list of countries that sanctioned the death penalty for juveniles.

Cognitively impaired—or mentally retarded—people face their own set of challenges within the justice system. In addition to having problems understanding the consequences of their actions, mentally retarded people often have problems instructing lawyers to defend them.

Many experts, as well as regular citizens, believe that youth and the mentally retarded face so many challenges within the justice system that it's impossible to ensure that their interests are fully protected. Those same critics believe that these individuals don't belong on death row.

The Death Penalty Information Center (DPIC) reports that between 1977 and the present, 22 individuals under the age of 18 at the time of their crimes have been executed in the United States. The youngest at the time of execution was Steven Roach. He was executed in Virginia in January 2000 at the age of 23. During the same period, DPIC reports 34 executions of individuals who showed evidence of mental retardation. Three prisoners, James Terry Roach, Dalton Prejean, and Johnny Frank Garrett, fell into both categories: they were under 18 at the time of the crime *and* mentally retarded.

In the summer of 2002, the U.S. Supreme Court ruled that it is unconstitutional to execute prisoners who are mentally retarded. Two years later, the same court ruled that it is unconstitutional to execute prisoners who were juveniles (under age 18) when they committed their crimes.

The age-related ruling came about as a result of the case of Christopher Simmons, a handsome blond teenager. Chris had been raised in a troubled home, and remained in conflict throughout his youth. His mother's second husband beat him, tied him to a tree, and forced him to drink alcohol against his will. Like many teenagers from abusive homes, Chris developed emotional problems (a schizotypal personality disorder) and a dependence on alcohol and marijuana that was established by the time he was 13.

When he was brought in for questioning for the brutal drowning murder of Shirley Crook, investigators suggested to Chris that confessing to the crime might spare him from death row. They lied.

Once behind bars, Chris became a model inmate, working with religious groups and programs designed to prevent teenagers from committing crimes. Teens touched by his efforts contributed to a groundswell of protest against his pending execution, and the efforts of lawyers, politicians, and mental health organizations to save Chris from execution ultimately led to the Supreme Court ruling that will ensure that no person will receive capital punishment for an offense committed before the age of 18.

Despite the sympathy about his case generated by his champions and defenders, we should remember that Chris committed a heinous crime. He was *not* innocent of binding and kidnapping his victim then pushing her off a bridge to her death.

* * *

However, not all juveniles who confess to violent crimes are guilty. The false promise of leniency that elicited Chris Simmons's confession is only one of the questionable tools that seasoned criminal investigators carry around in their psychological toolboxes. As we noted, a shocking percentage of teenaged suspects give *false* confessions when faced with pressure from police interrogators.

False confessions have enormous potential to lead to a wrongful conviction. Psychology professor Saul Kassin studied false confessions and noted that once suspects give police a signed confession, attempts to pursue other potential suspects virtually cease. Says Kassin: "Once in evidence, a confession is for all practical purposes a conviction."

Perhaps the most notorious example of the unreliability of youth confessions is the Central Park Five case. In that case, a 28-year-old white female jogger was raped, beaten, and left for dead in Central Park in 1989. The New York Police Department began an investigation, and quickly focused its attention on a group of young black boys. Two of the boys—Kevin Richardson and Raymond Santana—were 14 years old. Yusef Salaam and Antron McCray were 15. The eldest of the group was Kharey Wise, aged 16. McCray and Wise both had below-average

IQs, scoring 87 and 73, respectively.

The five boys had, by their own admission, been out on a night of substance abuse and mischief-making. Police picked them up and interrogated each of them for between 14 and 28 hours.

Each boy gave a videotaped statement confessing to having fondled and beaten a white woman that night. All five were convicted. They spent a combined total of 33 years in prison for the crime, with 14-year-old Raymond Santana serving the longest sentence, at eight years.

Thirteen years after the crime, Matias Reyes, a violent sex criminal already serving a 33-year sentence, became remorseful about something that had happened back in 1989. He confessed to the Central Park rape, and his confession was borne out by DNA testing of hairs left on the victim's body.

That was in 2002. By then, all five of the boys were young men in their early 20s, who had already served their sentences and been released—for a crime they didn't commit.

* * *

The Central Park Five case was tragic, but lucki-ly the victim didn't die, and the crime happened in New York State, which hasn't executed a pris-oner in more than 30 years.

The Four Heights Four—another group of young black men—had a much closer brush with state-sponsored execution.

In the wee hours of May 11, 1978, a filling station in Cook County, Illinois, was looted and robbed. The filling station was in Homewood, a mostly white neighborhood. The robbery hap-pened on the first day on the job for the over-night attendant, Larry Lionberg. He and his girl-friend, Carol Schmal, had just become engaged. Larry was 29 and Carol was 23. She was keeping Larry company at work that night.

Witnesses would later report seeing the couple abducted at gunpoint, and forced into a vehicle. They were taken to a predominantly black neighborhood, a 15-minute drive away. The next morning, two children discovered Larry Lionberg's body on a riverbank. He had been shot three times with a .38-calibre pistol. Carol was found less than an hour later on the second floor of a nearby townhouse. She was naked from the waist down, and had been shot twice in the head with the same gun. A later examination revealed that she had been raped.

The investigation was aided early on by an anonymous tipster, who called to report that the perpetrators were hanging around in the group of onlookers watching the police investigate the crime scene. The tipster told police to look for the drivers of a red Toyota and an orange Chevrolet. Spotting two young men walking towards a red Toyota, the police arrested Dennis Williams and Verneal Jimerson. Questioning of these first two men led to the subsequent arrests of two others: Willie Rainge and Kenny Adams. Rainge and Adams were friends of the first two suspects, and Adams owned a Chevrolet.

The anonymous tipster turned out to be Charles McCraney, who lived near the townhouse where Carol's body was found. He came forward and asked for police protection in return for information about the killings.

McCraney described a middle-of-the-night commotion on the street that ended with six to eight people running into the townhouse from the red and orange cars. He described hearing a single gunshot. When the police showed him some photographs, he identified three of the Ford Heights Four: Williams, Rainge, and Adams. He also mentioned that the police might be interested in speaking with a girl—17-year-old Paula Gray. Paula was a neighbor of McCraney's, and the girlfriend of Kenny Adams. IQ testing eventually revealed that Paula had an IQ of between 57 and 75, making her borderline mentally retarded.

When police approached Paula on May 13, two days after the murder, she told them that in the early hours of May 11, 1978, she had been with the Ford Heights Four at the townhouse when they raped Carol Schmal a total of seven times, and then shot her in the head. Paula explained that though the townhouse was in total darkness, she had watched the rapes and murder by the light of a Bic lighter. Once Carol was dead, said Paula, the men took Larry outside, walked him to the riverbank, shot him, then threw the gun into the creek and left his body there.

Paula retold her story before a grand jury on May 16, and all four men were charged with armed robbery, kidnapping, aggravated rape, and murder.

A month later at a pretrial hearing, Paula recanted, and said that her story had been made up. The court responded by charging her not only with perjury, but also with murder for her participation in the crime. Her recantation, however, meant that Verneal Jimerson could not be indicted; since McCraney had not identified him, there wasn't enough evidence to proceed without Paula's testimony.

The trial went ahead for the three men and Paula, with two juries—one for the men and one for Paula—sitting in the same courtroom. Even though Paula's confession had led to the indictment of the four men, she was represented by the same lawyer who represented Dennis Williams and Willie Rainge—an obvious conflict of interest.

Without Paula's confession, the prosecution was forced to scramble to come up with physical evidence. Hairs from the trunk of one of the cars were admitted on the grounds that they were "consistent with" Larry and Carol's hair. The jury was told that at least one of the rapists was a type A secretor—a blood type shared by 25 percent of the population, including Adams and Williams. Finally, the alibi witnesses for three of the four accused—Gray, Williams, and Adams—testified that the three were indeed hanging out on the street in front of Charles McCraney's house that night.

However, some of the puzzle pieces didn't fit. For one thing, investigators never found the murder weapon. Also, the alibi witnesses, who included the mothers of all four men, all testified that their sons had been at home in bed long before 3 a.m. Williams and Adams had been on the street outside McCraney's house—yes—but it was several hours *before* the timing of the commotion that McCraney had described to police.

But the juries found all four of the accused guilty.

Paula Gray was sentenced to 50 years in prison. Kenneth Adams got 75 years, and Willie Rainge was sentenced to life. Dennis Williams was sent to death row.

In the years that followed, Rainge and Williams earned the right to new trials, based on allegations that their defense lawyer had been incompetent. Paula Gray, changing her story again, agreed to testify against the two men in exchange for her freedom. Paula's co-operation meant that the prosecution could now charge Verneal Jimerson. All three men were convicted at the new trial.

Rainge and Adams stayed in jail. Jimerson joined Williams on death row.

But the verdicts didn't sit well with many in the community. The accused men's alibi witnesses continued to assert that they had been in their beds at the time of the crime. And, of course, there was the matter of Paula's confession, retraction, and new testimony.

The case attracted the interest of a Chicago journalist, Rob Warden, the editor and publisher of *Chicago Lawyer*, a legal affairs magazine. It also attracted the attention of David Protess, a journalism professor at Northwestern University. When they followed up on rumors that the Ford Heights Four were innocent, they discovered some troubling facts.

First, they learned that Paula's original confession had been obtained while the young girl was kept isolated by interrogators over two nights in suburban motels, sometimes with a gun to her head.

They learned that the jury that convicted Jimerson and affirmed the convictions of Williams and Rainge had never been told that Paula had been offered her freedom in exchange for her testimony at the second trial.

Finally, they learned that, a week after the crime, police had received—and done little to follow up on—a witness report stating that the wrong men had been arrested for the crime. According to this witness, four other men were responsible—he'd seen them flee the scene, and he'd seen them selling possessions stolen from the victims.

An eventual re-opening of the case implicated four completely different men: Dennis Johnson (who had since died), Ira Johnson, Arthur Robinson, and Juan Rodriguez. By the end of that investigation, DNA testing had established a match between Robinson's DNA and semen found in the body of Carol Schmal.

Ira Johnson, Robinson, and Rodriguez all confessed to the crime.

By 1996, all four of the Ford Heights Four were out of jail. They had served a combined total of over 65 years in prison, based largely on the coerced confession of a troubled, cognitively impaired 17-year-old girl. Dennis Williams died in March 2003 at the age of 46; he'd spent 18 of those 46 years in jail for a crime he didn't commit.

In March 1999, Cook County, Illinois, settled the men's compensation lawsuit for $36 million.

In 2001, Paula Gray was pardoned for her role in the prosecutions.

* * *

Despite the lessons learned in the Ford Heights Four case, where five wrongful convictions were built on the foundation of the confession of a cognitively impaired juvenile, mentally retarded accused continued to be sentenced to death row. In 1995, the state of Texas executed Mario Marquez, who had an IQ of 65, and, reportedly, "the adaptive skills of a 7-year-old."

In 2000, the state of Virginia pardoned Earl Washington, a man with an IQ of 69 who had spent 16 years in prison, 10 of them on death row. After being arrested on an unrelated charge, Washington, under pressure by investigators, falsely confessed to a 1982 rape and murder. DNA testing in 2000 excluded Washington from the list of possible perpetrators.

* * *

In 1989, the American Bar Association (ABA) spoke out against the death penalty for mentally retarded individuals. The persistence of several states in continuing to issue death sentences to cognitively impaired accused contributed to the ABA's call, in 1997, for a nationwide moratorium on the death penalty.

CHAPTER 6

Built on Lies: The Illinois Ten and Other Stories

hose who commit crimes often prey specifically on those who can least protect themselves, for example, children, the elderly, or women living alone. The death rows of the United States are populated, in large measure, by criminals whose crimes involved aggravating factors—such as unusual cruelty or disregard for human dignity—that provoked juries to sentence them to death.

Most people who seek careers within the justice system—such as police officers, lawyers, or judges—do so out of a sincere desire to protect the public from dangerous people. This desire motivates good police officers and prosecutors to hone and apply their investigative skills. It can also motivate the police to zero in as quickly as possible on potential suspects—a tendency that occasionally carries the risk of eliminating suspects prematurely. But most of the time, police and prosecutors do their work with care, compassion, and honesty.

But not *all* the time.

In a 1999 review of 62 exoneration cases, the Cardozo School of Law's Innocence Project found that police misconduct was a factor in a shocking 50 percent of cases, and misconduct on the part of prosecutors tainted 42 percent of cases.

While the sample was small, the evidence supports these statistics. Almost every case of

ERRORS LEADING TO WRONGFUL CONVICTION

In a 1999 study of 62 exoneration cases, the Cardozo Law School Innocence Project analyzed the factors leading to a wrongful conviction, and reported them as follows:

84%	mistaken eyewitnesses
50%	police misconduct
42%	prosecutorial misconduct
27%	incompetent defense lawyers
24%	false confessions
21%	lying snitches or informants

Source: Cardozo Law School Innocence Project

RELEASES FROM DEATH ROW SINCE 1973

Clemency or pardon with no evidence of innocence	218
Clemency with evidence of innocence	8
Full pardon based on innocence	7
All charges dismissed	72
Acquitted of all charges	43
Total	**348**

wrongful conviction reported by the Death Penalty Information Center documents actions by either police or prosecutors that appear to cross the line. Sometimes, police pursued the wrong suspect out of pure zeal or stubbornness; in other cases, members of the justice system turned a willfully blind eye to facts supporting an accused's innocence. In the worst cases, a conviction was built on outright, deliberate lies.

* * *

A case that has attracted particular outrage from critics is what has become known as the Jeanine Nicarico case, referred to by the media at the time as "the case that broke Chicago's heart."

On February 25, 1983, 10-year-old Jeanine Nicarico was alone at home, sick with the flu. Her mother, who worked nearby, rushed home on her lunch break to check on Jeanine. Then, Pat Nicarico returned to work.

At some point between Pat's departure

and Jeanine's sister, Kathy's, return home from school at 3 p.m., there was a knock on the door of the Nicarico house.

Jeanine, a friendly, dimpled little girl, went to the door in her nightgown. She called through the door to the visitor, saying she couldn't open the door because she was alone at home.

The intruder wouldn't take no for an answer. He kicked down the door. After raping and sodomizing Jeanine and crushing her skull with a blunt object, he left her body less than two miles (3 km) from her house. She'd been wrapped in a sheet, and a towel was taped over her eyes.

Leads in the case were slow in coming. The Chicago police announced a $10,000 reward for information leading to an arrest. With the crime still unsolved a year after its commission, the pressure was on the police department, because the county was in the middle of an election for the state's attorney.

A few days before the March 6, 1984, election, police announced the arrest of Rolando

Cruz, Alejandro Hernandez, and Stephen Buckley. The arrest came as a surprise to many members of the public, since no significant evidentiary breakthroughs had been reported.

Allegedly, the three young men had been making comments about having information about the crime. Alejandro Hernandez had given police the names of both Cruz and Buckley, and when Cruz was picked up, the police found him arrogant, boastful, and ready to talk about a version of the crime that he'd heard on the street.

Hernandez and Cruz may have simply been reckless braggarts, or they may have been motivated by the prospect of a $10,000 reward. Whatever their motivation, their testimony was going to have to be enough, because there was not a shred of physical evidence tying any of them to the crime.

When it came to Buckley, police took his boots as evidence to compare to a bootprint left on the Nicarico door. A criminologist in the sheriff's office concluded that Buckley's boot and the bootprint *were not* a match. The sheriff told the criminologist to keep his mouth shut. The sheriff's office shopped for a new expert and found one. Not only would she testify that the Buckley boot matched the print, but she claimed she could tell a person's height—and race—from their footprint.

The shaky case went to trial.

Michael Callahan, an insurance broker, was one of the jurors in the Cruz trial. In commenting about the trial afterwards, he said he felt that several of the jury members had their minds made up about the defendants' guilt before the trial even began. But after hearing the evidence, he was far from convinced: "I can remember vividly when the state's attorney rested his case, the thought in my mind was, 'This is all we're going to hear? I mean, this is it? This is the evidence?' I was just aghast. And I really started to feel uncomfortable."

Nevertheless, he succumbed to jury room pressure, and cast his guilty vote with the rest of the panel.

The jury was deadlocked over Buckley, but both Cruz and Hernandez were sentenced to death.

Unfortunately for the state, the conviction was overturned: the court found that it had been improper to try the three men together. So Cruz and Hernandez went to trial again, separately, this time. The charges against Buckley were dropped.

However, just before the Cruz trial was to begin, the prosecution was blessed with a stroke of luck. According to the prosecutor, two detectives had come forward with information they'd obtained just two months after the murder.

The detectives said they'd spoken with Cruz in May of 1983. There were no records of the interview—no videotape, no police notebook—but the detectives claimed that they remembered listening to Cruz recount a vision in which he could see Jeanine at the time of her murder. She had a broken nose, Cruz had said, and she had hit her head so hard it left a mark on the ground.

Strangely, not only did the detectives not make notes of this "vision" conversation, but they let Cruz walk free after hearing it. When it came time to testify at the grand jury the vision confession wasn't mentioned in the testimony of either detective. Cruz wasn't asked about it either.

The defense smelled a rat and scrambled to have evidence pertaining to the vision interview excluded from the trial. The judge didn't buy it, and the evidence was presented to the jury.

The prosecution was successful again, although this time only Cruz received a capital sentence. Hernandez was sentenced to 80 years in prison.

Two months later, while the two convicts were safely tucked away in prison, another little girl disappeared in LaSalle County, an hour's drive from the Nicarico home. This girl, Melissa Ackerman, was only seven. Like Jeanine, Melissa was carried from her home wrapped in bedding. She was taken to a wooded area where she was sodomized and murdered.

Melissa's murder investigation proceeded more quickly. The police arrested a man named Brian Dugan and began negotiating with him about how he would plead in the case. Dugan agreed to plead guilty not only to Melissa's murder, but to the murder of two other females: 27-year-old Donna Schnorr and Jeanine Nicarico.

Police finally had their direct confession. Except it wasn't from Cruz or Hernandez, the two men who were serving time for the murder.

The LaSalle County police called the DuPage County prosecutors—the ones responsible for Jeanine's case. DuPage County sent Robert Kilander, the first assistant, and another young prosecutor to LaSalle County to talk with Dugan's lawyer. But when the two prosecutors returned home to Chicago, they refused to pursue the Dugan matter further.

Bemused, the LaSalle prosecutors made another call—this time to the Illinois State

Police. The state police investigated the matter of Dugan's confession and quickly concluded that the wrong men were in prison. Not only had Dugan confessed, but he knew details of the crime that were not public knowledge. His car tires matched a tire mark that had been found near Jeanine's body. He had missed work on the day of Jeanine's murder and had been seen a couple of blocks from her house.

The state police contacted the prosecutor's office with what they knew, but the prosecutors stood firm. They were leaving Dugan alone. No call about the Dugan confession was ever made to Cruz's and Hernandez's lawyers. Two investigators from the sheriff's office eventually resigned in disgust over the failure to follow up on the Dugan confession.

Cruz and Hernandez appealed again. The prosecution's side of the appeal was first assigned to prosecutor Mary Brigid Kenney, but Kenney refused to do it. She didn't believe that the convictions should be preserved, and she resigned on principle. The prosecution assigned another lawyer, who lost the appeal. Cruz and Hernandez were granted a third trial after their convictions were vacated—not because another man had confessed, but because of some procedural irregularities. They would have to be tried yet again.

For the third Cruz trial, the prosecution came up with a new witness, one who would corroborate the troubling "vision interview" evidence. The witness was a lieutenant in the police department, and he was supposed to say that he had received a call from the interviewing investigators, who'd asked him for advice about what to do about the statement.

But when the lieutenant was put on the stand, he admitted that he'd lied to the prosecution. He'd never received any such call. In fact, he was in Florida on holiday at the time.

The judge ended the trial on the spot. He refused to convict Cruz or Hernandez a third time. Ten years after they were first convicted, and 10 years after Brian Dugan had confessed to the murder, the two men were free to go.

Later, DNA testing linked Brian Dugan to the rape and murder of Jeanine Nicarico.

The handling of the Nicarico case outraged even people within the justice system. In 1998, a special prosecutor was appointed to thoroughly review the case. Four investigators from the sheriff's office and three prosecutors were charged with perjury and obstruction of justice. Although the charges didn't stick, the message had been sent: fakery, cover-ups, and lies would no longer be tolerated in Illinois when the lives of innocent people were at stake.

* * *

Fast on the heels of the exonerations of Cruz and Hernandez came the matter of Steve Manning.

Manning was also on death row in Illinois. He was a former police officer who was kicked off the force after being convicted of taking part in a jewelry heist. His connections with both law enforcement and the criminal element made him useful, however: after he got out of jail for the robbery, he became an informant for the FBI.

In 1990, James Pellegrino, an ex-business partner of Manning, turned up dead. The state presented a statement from Pellegrino's wife implicating Manning, but there was no real evidence linking Manning to the slaying. To boost their case, prosecutors made a deal with a jail-house snitch named Thomas Dye. In exchange for implicating Manning, Dye's own sentence would be reduced from 14 to 6 years.

Dye came through, telling prosecutors that Manning had confessed. Dye also invited Manning to collaborate with his girlfriend, Sylvia Herrera, to concoct an alibi for another crime in which Manning had been implicated: a kidnapping in the state of Missouri six years earlier.

The kidnapping charges were filed just days before Manning's arrest for murder. Manning would later sue the FBI, alleging that he had been set up for refusing to continue to co-operate as an informant.

The Missouri kidnapping trial happened first. As planned by the FBI, Sylvia Herrera be-trayed Manning, testifying on behalf of the prosecution about Manning's efforts to con-coct a fake alibi. The first trial failed, ending in a hung jury. The second time around, the Mis-souri prosecutors won, and Manning was sen-tenced to two concurrent life terms plus 100 years. He still had a murder trial to go through, in the neighboring state of Illinois.

At the murder trial, the prosecution allowed Mrs. Pellegrino to testify that her husband had said, essentially, "If I turn up dead, call the FBI and tell them Manning killed me."

They also put Thomas Dye on the stand. His testimony was less effective, because while he said that Manning had confessed, six hours of tapes of his conversations with Manning failed to produce any admissions of guilt in the

Pellegrino matter. But it was enough for the jury. In 1993, Manning was sentenced to die for the Pellegrino murder.

In 1998, Manning argued, on appeal, that it was inappropriate for the jury to have heard Mrs. Pellegrino's hearsay testimony or the jail-house tapes. The snitch tapes, his lawyer argued, were highly prejudicial: they didn't contain a confession, but they did make Manning look bad, because of the mention of his involvement in unrelated crimes.

The court agreed and ordered a new trial. In 2000, the prosecution chose not to retry Manning; they dropped the charges instead.

* * *

Manning became the 13th person to walk off death row since Illinois reinstated the death penalty in 1977. The statistic didn't sit well with George Ryan, the state governor.

Why? Between 1977 and 2000, the number of people executed in Illinois stood at 12. With Manning's exoneration, which came in the midst of a flurry of allegations of corruption in the Illinois justice system, the number of people exonerated had *outstripped* the number of people executed.

George Ryan had always been in favor of capital punishment. He believed in the system, especially when a neighbor of his was abducted and buried alive, landing the perpetrator on his state's death row. But the things he had seen and heard while in the governor's office had begun to give him pause. Cruz and Hernandez had served years on death row, even after the real killer had confessed. Now Manning, fingered by a jailhouse snitch, was suing the FBI. Maybe the system wasn't so perfect after all. Maybe it couldn't be trusted, when the stakes were life or death. In a speech just before his retirement from office in 2003, Ryan publicly declared: "[I]f we haven't got a system that works, then we shouldn't have a system."

But the first indications of his change of heart came three years earlier, in January 2000. On the heels of Manning's exoneration, Governor Ryan took the extraordinary step of declaring a moratorium on all executions in the state of Illinois. "Until I can be sure, with moral certainty, that no innocent man or woman is facing a lethal injection," Ryan said, "no one will meet that fate."

Three years later, days before his retirement and with that moral certainty still out of his reach, Ryan pardoned four more inmates: Aaron Patterson, Madison Hobley, Stanley Howard, and Leroy Orange. Three of the four men had maintained that their confessions had been elicited through police torture.

But Ryan found he still couldn't sleep at night. On the eve of his retirement, he left his final legacy: the remaining inmates on Illinois's death row—all 164 of them—would have their death sentences commuted to life in prison. Bill Kurtis wrote, of this extraordinary act:

"... [George Ryan] chose to sign off [from his term as governor] as a whistle-blower, knowing he would be pilloried by relatives of the victims of death-row inmates, death penalty proponents, and many in law enforcement. He most likely did not know he would also be nominated for the Nobel Peace Prize, and would win praise from governments and individuals around the world. Either way, his decision to speak out instead of remaining quiet was an act of immense courage."

* * *

Illinois and its ex-governor have become emblematic of America's uneasy relationship with capital punishment. It would be easy for those who support the death penalty to dismiss the Illinois experience as an aberration—an isolated case of corruption, now corrected.

To think that, however, we would have to ignore a key research finding. In his famous study of error rates in U.S. capital cases, James Liebman found the rate of error in Illinois cases to be 66 percent. That's two percentage points *lower* than the national average of 68 percent.

CHAPTER 7

Champions of the Unpopular

Statistics routinely suggest that when it comes to the death penalty, U.S. public opinion is volatile. An October 2005 Gallup poll noted that overall support for capital punishment had dropped to 64 percent, the lowest it's been since 1978. Just nine years earlier, however, support for state-sanctioned execution had reached an all-time high of 80 percent.

The death penalty has always been a

political hot button; entire political campaigns, in some jurisdictions, have turned on pro-death penalty platforms. And while Republicans are slightly more likely to support capital punishment, leaders of major parties are wise to tiptoe around the issue: death penalty supporters form a majority of voters in both camps.

Speaking out against the death penalty and questioning the system that imposes it have never been popular. Most of the men and women on America's death row have earned their places there by committing crimes that shock.

But there is something about fighting for the *innocent* that strikes a more favorable chord. Not even those who are ideologically committed to the death penalty are willing to contemplate the execution of innocents. It's a disgrace to the system.

In October 2004, President George W. Bush signed into law a bill called the Justice For All Act (JFAA), that promotes the rights of victims and criminal accused.

The Innocence Protection Act (IPA), part of the JFAA, provides a legal framework for three important objectives. First, it creates guidelines for access to DNA testing for federal offenders who allege "actual innocence"; second, it creates a grant program through which states can seek federal funding to improve their prosecution and public defender systems for capital crimes; and third, it increases the level of compensation that the government will pay to wrongfully convicted federal offenders to $50,000 per year for wrongful imprisonment for non-capital crimes, and $100,000 for wrongful imprisonment for capital crimes.

Chairman of the House Judiciary Committee—F. James Sensenbrenner—and Representative William Delahunt introduced the JFAA bill into the House. The bill, a collaborative, bipartisan effort led by Senate Judiciary Chairman Orrin Hatch and Senator Patrick Leahy, represents a step in the right direction at least for those inmates on federal death row.

* * *

Legislative innovations, such as the JFAA, often result from political pressure. As one of a handful of developed countries that retains the death penalty, the United States faces considerable pressure from international bodies, like the United Nations, to eliminate the death penalty, or at least to stop the wrongful conviction of innocent people.

Individual countries apply similar pressure. The United States' northern neighbor, Canada, abolished the death penalty decades ago. Mexico, to the south, theoretically allows capital punishment for exceptional crimes such as high treason, but has not executed a prisoner since 1937. The Mexican government issued the following statement in 1997: "[T]he death penalty puts an end to the enjoyment of the right to life, which is the most fundamental human prerogative, as universally recognized in such legal instruments as the Universal Declaration of Human Rights. It is a cruel, inhuman and degrading sentence and has been demonstrated to serve absolutely no deterrent function, which is why Mexico has joined in international efforts towards its abolition and is in favor of all measures to that end."

Countries that have abolished the death penalty sometimes express their opposition to U.S. retention of the practice by refusing to extradite criminals wanted for capital crimes in the United States.

Finally, some high-profile humanitarian organizations around the world, such as Amnesty International, have for years expressed their dismay with a U.S. system that makes, in their view, too many mistakes.

* * *

Amnesty International USA has long been an opponent of the death penalty in general. The organization writes: "Amnesty International unconditionally opposes the death penalty under all circumstances. Every death sentence is an affront to human dignity: the ultimate form of cruel, inhuman and degrading punishment. Each execution is a violation of the most fundamental human right: the right to life itself."

The risk of execution of *innocent* people creates an even stronger incentive for abolition, according to the organization. It notes that "[t]he likelihood that innocent people will be condemned to death and executed is inherent in all jurisdictions which resort to capital punishment" and argues that "[t]he undeniable fact that the death penalty is sometimes inflicted upon those innocent of the crime for which they were condemned only reinforces the other conclusive arguments against its use."

* * *

On American soil, myriad political and humanitarian organizations work to publicize the anti-death penalty cause and to raise awareness of the execution of innocent prisoners. An example of a recent political initiative is the "1000 Executions" project, a coalition of the American Civil Liberties Union, Amnesty International USA, Citizens United for Alternatives to the Death Penalty, Death Penalty Focus, National Coalition to Abolish the Death Penalty, and Virginians for Alternatives to the Death Penalty. The 1,000th American execution since the 1976 reinstatement of the death penalty occurred on December 2, 2005, at 2 a.m.

The dubious honor of being the 1,000th person executed fell to Kenneth Boyd, who died by lethal injection in North Carolina.

* * *

Another well-known quasi-political opponent of the death penalty is the Roman Catholic Church. The official position of the Catholic Church is that capital punishment is wrong.

A teaching about capital punishment offered by the American Catholic Bishops includes the statement that "abolition of capital punishment is ... a manifestation of our belief in the unique worth and dignity of each person from the moment of conception, a creature made in the image and likeness of God." The Catholic Church believes that this basic tenet of respect for life extends even to those who have taken life.

Pope John Paul II made many statements during his papal tenure in support of the abolition of capital punishment. He directed his mercy to the plight of individual prisoners as well. In a visit to St. Louis, he persuaded then-governor Mel Carnahan to exercise clemency in commuting the sentence of murderer Darrell Mease, who had been scheduled for execution on the day of the papal visit.

This strong stance against the death penalty has encouraged a number of innocents to appeal to the Church for support in obtaining exonerations, and the Church has listened. For example, the Pope intervened on behalf of Joaquin Martinez, who was cleared, acquitted, and freed from death row in 2001. When Governor George Ryan commuted all Illinois death-row sentences in 2003, the Pope responded with an official statement of support and praise.

Perhaps the best-known individual religious figure to make a name for herself as a champion of the innocent is Sister Helen Prejean, the author of *Dead Man Walking*, a book on which a successful film and opera was based. The prisoner in that book was guilty of his crimes. Sister Prejean's latest book, *The Death of Innocents: an Eyewitness Account of Wrongful Executions*, details the struggles of two prisoners executed despite Sister Prejean's belief in their innocence. The story of Dobie Gillis Williams, executed in Prejean's home state of Louisiana, is particularly compelling. Junk science, an entrenched "old boys'" network, and overt racism marred Mr. Williams's arrest, trial, and sentence.

Sister Prejean reserves particular anger for

the racism that taints the administration of the death penalty in the United States. In commenting on the factors that influence the imposition of death sentences, she argues that it's not adjectives about the crime—such as cruel or premeditated—that influence who will get life and who will get death, but rather nouns. The decision to hand down a death sentence is guided, according to Prejean, by "who was killed and who did the killing. Since Gregg [a legal decision that set sentencing guidelines], 8 out of every 10 persons executed for murder had white victims."

Sister Prejean continues in her efforts to obtain a posthumous exoneration of Dobie Gillis Williams and Joseph O'Dell, and to work with the wrongfully convicted and the families of murder victims. In a speech in Philadelphia in 1999, she concluded with the following:

> *I think the death penalty simply epitomizes the three deepest wounds we have*

in our society. One is the racism that riddles it. Mostly it's when white people get killed that the death penalty is even sought. Racism is in this thing inside and out. Our penchant for choosing the poor to pay the ultimate price and to suffer the harshest punishments, to make them the scapegoats—that's another wound. The third is our penchant for trying to solve our social problems with military solutions. The death penalty is one more military solution: target an enemy, dehumanize the enemy, and kill the enemy. The book of Deuteronomy says, "Look, I set before you death and life. Choose life."

Other religious organizations are of mixed opinions about the death penalty. While no religion would support the knowing execution of innocents; conservative, fundamental, or evangelical religions are more likely than their more

liberal counterparts to support the death penalty. Where a religion has both conservative and
liberal branches (for example, Judaism), support for the death penalty is often split along
these lines.

* * *

Political and religious opposition, however, usually offers only generalized hope. For individual
innocent prisoners, the slow and steady forces
of political will are not enough to loosen the
bonds that hold them individually. Other, more
personalized, efforts are needed.

While supporters of capital punishment argue that 122 exonerations since 1973 mean that
the justice system is working—innocent people
are being saved from execution—innocents
such as Gary Gauger argue that it's the opposite.
"I was not exonerated because of the system. I
was exonerated in spite of the system. If it was
up to the prosecution, they would still try to ex-

ecute me," asserts Gauger.

Gauger got off death row with the help of the Innocence Project.

One of the greatest risks to innocent prisoners is inertia on the part of both politicians and the courts. If politicians feel that it would not play well in the media to grant an inmate clemency, they will often assert that they are not willing to second guess the findings of the justice system. This is what happened in 1997 when lawyers for Kevin Byrd approached George W. Bush, then-governor of Texas, with compelling evidence that Byrd was innocent. Bush, who is famous for being unwilling to exercise clemency while governor, refused, saying the matter was up to the courts, not politicians, to resolve.

But the courts, in turn, often take a similar hands-off approach. Jackson and colleagues, in their book *Legal Lynching: The Death Penalty and America's Future,* argue that "the U.S. Supreme Court has raised the practice of execution by technicality to an art form." They cite

the 1992 decision not to intervene in the case
of Lionel Herrera, whose brother confessed to
the crime for which Lionel had been convicted.
In his reasons declining to help Herrera, Chief
Justice Rehnquist wrote "[h]istory shows that
the traditional remedy for claims of innocence
based on new evidence ... has been executive
clemency."

Faced with a justice system that won't
budge and politicians who won't intervene, innocent prisoners find themselves in dire need of
a champion: someone who will speak for them.

It was this desperation that inspired two
lawyers, Barry Scheck and Peter Neufeld, to establish the Innocence Project at New York's Benjamin N. Cardozo School of Law in 1992.

Scheck and Neufeld met in 1977, while
working at Bronx Legal Aid. At the time, New
York's Bronx neighborhood was dirt poor and
riddled with crime. The lawyers who gravitated
there to work long hours for rotten pay did so
out of deep-seated convictions about issues

such as social justice and racial equality. Scheck and Neufeld were no exceptions.

Barry Scheck was the Yale-educated son of an entertainment mogul, but he had radical ideas and wasn't afraid to share them as a debater and political activist.

Peter Neufeld came from a family of humanitarians; his mother was a leader in the Ethical Culture movement, and his brother was a leader in the largest anti-Vietnam War student protest movement. Peter was thrown out of school more than once for his own anti-war activism.

The two men had radically different styles. In their book, *Actual Innocence: Five Days from Execution and Other Dispatches from the Wrongly Convicted*, written with journalist Jim Dwyer, they describe the contrast as follows: "[I]f they were ever trying to escape from a jail, Peter would drive a high-powered truck through the wall. Barry would talk the guard into lending him keys for the night."

After they'd both left Legal Aid for private practice, Scheck and Neufeld found themselves together again when they were asked to handle the case of Marion Coakley, a disruptive, mentally challenged—but innocent—prisoner convicted of rape. Coakley had been shuttled back and forth around the New York state prison system because of his disruptive and destructive behavior. But the Legal Aid lawyers who had first clumsily represented him were convinced of his innocence.

So was a lab technician who had conducted preliminary tests on physical evidence—a rape kit—collected in the case. The evidence was excluded when the case went to trial, because the technician had waffled on its meaning. But when Scheck and Neufeld interviewed him, the technician said he believed that a brand-new kind of testing, one that could produce a genetic "fingerprint" of an offender, would probably show that Coakley was innocent of the crime.

At the time—1987—DNA science was in its

infancy; the first prisoner to be exonerated by DNA evidence would not happen for another two years.

The fancy lab suggested by the Bronx lab technician was Lifecodes—the only one in the United States that could analyze DNA evidence at the time. Unfortunately, it was unable to produce a DNA profile in the Coakley case. What was worse, in the process of trying, the lab had used up what was left of the physical evidence in the case.

It was a setback, but undeterred, Scheck and Neufeld and the two dedicated law students they'd recruited to help them managed to convince the unruly prisoner to provide not one, but 13 semen samples. Using these samples, the lawyers were able, based on more primitive serological (bodily secretions) analysis, to prove that Coakley was innocent. He walked out of jail a free man.

While it hadn't been a factor in their success in the Coakley case, Scheck and Neufeld had had their first brush with DNA science, and they were inspired. Almost 20 years later, their enthusiasm has proven to be well-placed: by their count, DNA analysis has led to the exoneration of at least 163 wrongly convicted individuals, including 14 who were serving time on death row.

In 1992, Scheck and Neufeld founded the Innocence Project. The project is dedicated to working on behalf of the wrongfully convicted. It faces overwhelming demand, with a backlog of thousands of applicants for its services. The Innocence Project has been forced, by sheer volume of demand, to restrict access to its program to those cases in which the convicted person alleges that post-conviction DNA testing will prove his or her innocence.

Access to the help of Innocence Projects is limited, with thousands of prisoners competing for donated time and resources, as time ticks on the clock. This level of competition means that some prisoners will continue to fall through the cracks. Luckily, other organizations work tire-lessly on behalf of these unpopular clients. For example, the Louisiana Crisis Assistance Center (now the Louisiana Capital Assistance Center) helped match Louisiana death-row prisoner John Thompson with the two Philadelphia commercial lawyers who worked on his case, *pro bono*, for 15 years.

The efforts of individual lawyers, such as Thompson's Michael L. Banks and Gordon Cooney Jr., and journalists like Rob Warden (who worked on the Ford Heights Four and many other cases), and of their dozens of tire-less students, researchers, and foot soldiers, form the real heart of the struggle to get inno-cent people off death row.

CHAPTER 8

The Death Penalty Debate

I t's impossible to consider ways to prevent the incarceration and execution of innocent people without considering the appropriateness of the death penalty in general. Almost everyone agrees that the execution of innocent people is an intolerable blot on the reputation of the U.S. justice system.

What garners less agreement, however, is the suggestion that the system will inevitably execute some innocents.

The reasons innocent people are sometimes convicted of capital crimes are varied and complex. According to the famous Liebman study, it takes on average three judicial examinations, including appeals, for most errors to be uncovered, if they are uncovered at all.

Proponents of the death penalty argue that 122 death-row exonerations since 1973 mean that the system works: the mistakes are coming to light, and innocent people are being set free. Most exonerees, however, feel that they are alive despite the system, and that they can never be adequately compensated for the hard years that they and their families spent waiting for death.

Do the benefits of the death penalty outweigh the burden of a little innocent blood on the system's hands? The question can't be answered unless we know two things: that the death penalty does benefit society and that the system is guilty of wrongful killing in our names.

Arguments for the Death Penalty

The most important pro-death penalty arguments are that the death penalty is a deterrent, and that it provides justice to families who have lost loved ones at the hands of violent killers. But there are also less frequently cited arguments.

One of those is cost: the first executions by gas chamber at San Quentin Prison in California were conducted in 1938. Two prisoners, Robert Lee Cannon and Albert Kassell, were executed at the same time, and the cost to the government for the necessary cyanide was just $1.80.

Modern executions are almost always by lethal injection, and this, too, is an inexpensive undertaking; the drugs used are commonly available pharmaceuticals.

Even when you include the cost of incarcerating prisoners for an average of 12 years before they are executed, capital punishment appears to cost considerably less than imprisonment for life without parole.

Unfortunately, the apparent cost advantage of execution doesn't hold water. The reason for this has nothing to do with the cost of killing prisoners, or of housing them in prisons for life. Instead, it has to do with legal costs.

When a person is charged with a capital crime, the legal bills—most of which are paid by the state on both sides, since most capital murderers cannot afford lawyers—begin to pile up immediately. Some studies have suggested that the cost of obtaining a death sentence, and defending that sentence through the usual course of appeals that are brought between sentencing and execution, is about $2.2 million per convict. Experts suggest that this is more than it would cost to convict the same person of non-capital murder and to house him in prison for 100 years.

Another cost issue is compensation for the wrongfully convicted. When a person is sentenced to death and then later exonerated, the state is exposed to claims for compensation. The Ford Heights Four settled their civil suit against

Cook County, Illinois, for $36 million. The Innocence Protection Act, passed in 2004, raised the statutory compensation for federal death-row exonerees to $100,000 per year of wrongful imprisonment.

A second benefit cited by some death penalty supporters is religious justice. Some fundamentalist and conservative religions support capital punishment. The Bible's Old Testament contains a famous reference to taking "an eye for an eye" and similar forms of punishment appear in other religious texts, such as the Koran.

Unfortunately, religious arguments in favor of the death penalty are problematic in a diverse, democratic society such as the United States. A wide range of religions are practiced and tolerated in the United States, but only a minority of those espouse a clear pro-capital punishment mandate. And within the same faith, support for capital punishment is often split between different branches.

Finally, because it is impossible to prove

that the execution of criminals pleases God, Allah, or any other religious entity, it is impossible to prove that capital punishment provides religious justice.

The last of the second-tier arguments in favor of the death penalty is incapacitation. If a convict is dead, he or she can never kill again. However, a sentence of life in prison without parole—the sentence most commonly suggested as an alternative to capital punishment—achieves the same goal, presuming there is no possibility for escape.

Also, incapacitation, as an argument, is an implicit rejection of rehabilitation. While not all offenders can be successfully rehabilitated, murder is a crime with a low repeat offending rate: convicted murderers are *less* likely, upon release, to commit murder than are people released after being imprisoned for other crimes.

The two remaining arguments in favor of capital punishment—deterrence and retribution—are by far the most powerful.

A groundbreaking study by Isaac Ehrlich in 1975 used statistical theory to document a connection between the use of the death penalty and the murder rate between 1933 and 1970. Ehrlich suggested that, based on his data each execution deterred about eight homicides.

> **QUOTE**
>
> "Why ... does the deterrence myth persist? Police know the death penalty doesn't deter crime. Crime-policy experts know it. The scholars know it. It is only politicians, it seems, who have not heard the news."
>
> *Rev. Jesse L. Jackson*

Unfortunately, in the years that followed, other scientists were unable to replicate Ehrlich's results, or to isolate a deterrent factor associated with the death penalty. Some retentionist states have higher murder rates than their abolitionist neighbors. In some states, abolition of the death penalty has been followed by a drop in the murder rate. Many countries with no death penalty—for example, Canada and the United Kingdom—have much lower murder rates than the United States. Finally, surveys of law enforcement professionals in both the United States and Canada have shown that the police themselves tend not to believe that the availability of the death penalty deters criminality.

Of course, it's impossible to say with any certainty that the U.S. murder rate would not be even higher if there were no death penalty; but the lack of evidence in support of deterrence suggests that if the death penalty has a deterrent effect, it's a very modest one.

The last argument in favor of the death penalty has been described as retribution, vengeance, or moral justice.

However you describe it, retribution is the pro-death penalty argument with the widest base of support. A 1996 study by Jennifer Honeyman and James R. P. Ogloff found a correlation between high scores on a "Vengeance Scale" and the likelihood that a test subject would recommend the death penalty after listening to the description of a murder scenario.

The word "vengeance" has negative connotations to some, and many death-penalty supporters prefer to describe retribution in terms of moral justice. Those who support the death penalty on the basis of retributive justice strongly believe that murderers "deserve" to suffer the same fate as their victims.

Strongly held pro-death-penalty beliefs are difficult to shake. The Honeyman and Ogloff study suggested that individuals who support the death penalty as a suitable sentence for some crimes are very unlikely to be swayed from that position by any anti-death penalty arguments. In U.S. retentionist states, jurors in capital cases typically have to be "death-qualified," which means that jurors who oppose the death penalty on principle can be excluded from serving on a capital jury because they are unwilling to impose one of the possible available sentences.

Studies such as the Honeyman and Ogloff one suggest that talking jurors out of the death penalty by raising anti-death-penalty arguments is probably a futile strategy for defense attorneys. Honeyman and Ogloff cite an earlier study for the proposition that support for capital punishment is more moral and emotional than rational: "[I]t has been suggested ... that a person's position on the issue of capital punishment is not determined by a rational evaluation of the arguments for and against the death penalty, but is an emotionally based, moral opinion, that may be based on vengeance."

Not everybody, however, equates moral justice with the death penalty, and not everybody believes in the value of retribution. It is not uncommon for family members of murder victims to speak out against capital punishment for their loved ones' convicted killers. This phenomenon is most common in cases where there is doubt about the innocence of the prisoner. For example, in the Larry Griffin case, members of the victim's family lent their support to the NAACP's attempts to open the investigation.

In some cases, a rejection of retribution as an appropriate goal for the justice system has its roots in religious beliefs. Sister Helen Prejean believes that the Roman Catholic Church values respect for human life well above retribution for human wrongs. She cautions against the substitution of legal justice for moral justice, saying that "laws have a way of legitimating prejudice, which unleashes brutality even in normally mild, respectable citizens." Her view and that of most modern churches, however, is a minority view. Support for the death penalty fluctuates between 60 and 80 percent in the absence of solid evidence that the death penalty is a deterrent, suggesting that most Americans believe in retributive justice.

Arguments against the Death Penalty

Besides seeking to refute the usual pro-capital punishment arguments—in particular, economics and deterrence—anti-capital punishment supporters tend to suggest five main arguments for abolition:

1. Vengeance is an inappropriate goal for a modern justice system.
2. Capital punishment is cruel and unusual punishment.
3. The death penalty is applied arbitrarily, and hence unfairly.
4. Capital punishment is brutal, and begets brutality in society at large.
5. The system makes too many mistakes for us to trust it with life-or-death decisions.

The first two issues have already been discussed in this book. That leaves the topics of arbitrariness, societal influence, and mistake.

Arbitrariness—the uneven and unpredictable application of the death penalty—was one of the concerns at the root of the 1972 decision in *Furman v. Georgia.* That decision led to a ruling that capital punishment, as it was being applied in the United States, was unconstitutional. The *Furman* decision led to a nationwide moratorium on executions, which was unbroken until another legal decision—1976's *Gregg v. Georgia*—made it possible for states to re-introduce the death penalty as long as appropriate guidelines for sentencing were established.

However, strong evidence suggests that the *Gregg* guidelines did not remedy the problem of arbitrariness in the application of the death penalty. The Death Penalty Information Center notes that: "[T]here remains a lack of uniformity in the capital punishment system. Some of the most heinous murders do not result in death sentences, while less heinous crimes are punished by death ... Many factors other than the gravity of the crime or the culpability of the offender appear to affect death sentences, including geography, race, gender, and access to adequate counsel."

The following statistics and anecdotes support this conclusion:

- Baltimore City had only one person on Maryland's death row, but suburban Baltimore

County, with one-tenth the number of murders as the city, had nine times the number on
death row (Montgomery, 2002).

• The death penalty is imposed much more often in southern U.S. states than it is in northern U.S. states, regardless of the crime rate in
the relevant state.

Simply living in the suburbs, living in the
South, or murdering a white person instead
of a person of color are clearly not factors that
should be allowed to increase a person's risk of
receiving the death penalty.

The arbitrariness of death sentences is a
problem that the legal system appears incapa-
ble of solving; and opponents of the death penalty believe that capital punishment that is arbitrary—as well as racist and stacked against the
poor—is not only unfair, but unconstitutional.

The fourth anti-death-penalty argument is
perhaps the most subtle; but not too subtle to
be understood by most countries in the Euro-

pean Union and many other parts of the world. Many people and their governments believe that a government's retention of the death penalty sets an unacceptable example for citizens. The death penalty, these opponents say, is brutal and backward, and a government's willingness to execute its own nationals sends a message to the people that brutality and killing are acceptable. The death penalty flies in the face of respect for human life, a value that is at the core of many rehabilitation programs.

Many inmates on death row hold the notion that the death penalty amounts to state-sanctioned vengeance and barbarism. Instead of viewing execution as "just deserts" for their crimes, and feeling remorse, many death-row inmates turn their anger toward the executioner and view the state as no less criminal than the murderers it executes. Bobby Ray Hopkins, an outspoken prisoner who was executed in Texas on February 12, 2004, wrote of the system that would kill him: "No one is willing to take responsibility for the darkened bloodstains that are on their hands and embedded deep down within their hearts and minds as well."

And for the innocent people on death row—those who have not themselves committed murder—the state's brutality must seem particularly repugnant.

Many law-abiding citizens share the view that the death penalty is brutal and bad for society, even though they have lost loved ones to murder. Coretta Scott King, the late wife of Dr. Martin Luther King Jr., maintained a staunch anti-death-penalty stance even after her husband and mother-in-law were assassinated: "I stand firmly and unequivocally opposed to the death penalty for those convicted of capital offenses. An evil deed is not redeemed by an evil deed of retaliation. Justice is never advanced in the taking of a human life. Morality is never upheld by a legalized murder."

A less famous survivor, Marietta Jaeger, had the following, more personal message, when faced with the prospect of execution for the murderer of her seven-year-old daughter, Susie: "My own daughter was such a gift of joy and sweetness and beauty, that to kill someone in her name would have been to violate and profane the goodness of her life; the idea is offensive and repulsive to me."

The final argument made against capital punishment forms the central theme of this book: it is impossible to know, with moral certainty, that the system reliably spares the lives of innocent people. James Liebman's groundbreaking research suggests that serious, reversible errors occurred in nearly 7 out of 10 capital sentences issued in the United States between 1973 and 1995. Samuel Gross and his colleagues, having studied wrongful convictions between 1989 and 2003, found evidence to support the proposition that errors are *more* likely to occur in capital cases than in other cases.

But no statistic is more powerful than the 122 death-row exonerations across the nation in just 29 years. Most of those exonerations have been achieved only after Herculean efforts by dedicated lawyers, journalists, students, and family members.

The suggestion that the system is infallible—that no innocent people are ever put to death—is not reasonable, based on the evidence of 122 exonerations. Not all convicts have access to the legal representation and post-conviction DNA testing that could potentially free them, even given unlimited time. Appeals are limited to the review of legal issues, and are of no use in cases where a juror is swayed by a lying witness, comes to an irrational conclusion in spite of the evidence, or is motivated by blind revenge. And studies of eyewitness testimony continue to prove that it is possible for good, honest human beings to be absolutely certain of a fact, or of an identification, and still be absolutely wrong.

After reviewing two exoneration cases, journalist Bill Kurtis—once a supporter of the death penalty—had the following to say: "... there are hundreds of tiny decisions made in the course of investigation and trial that can easily be wrong as they are right … what those many tiny decisions show us is the fragility of the system. The administration of justice is complicated, too complicated to make death its product."

* * *

The United States' track record in convicting, imprisoning, and sometimes exonerating innocent accused leads inevitably to the conclusion expressed by U.S. District Judge Michael Ponsor: "A legal regime relying on the death penalty will inevitably execute innocent people—not too often, one hopes, but undoubtedly sometimes. Mistakes will be made because it is simply not possible to do something this difficult perfectly, all the time. Any honest proponent of capital punishment must face this fact."

After facing this fact, and the knowledge that capital punishment is not applied consistently, and is neither less expensive nor a better deterrent than a sentence of life in prison, is it reasonable to retain the death penalty? The answer depends on whether you believe that putting accused murderers—most of whom are guilty, but some of whom are not—to death for their crimes benefits the society in which you live. As many who have studied motivations for capital punishment recognize, the answer to that question depends heavily on how highly we value vengeance, and how many innocent human lives we are willing to sacrifice in the name of retribution.

A Timeline

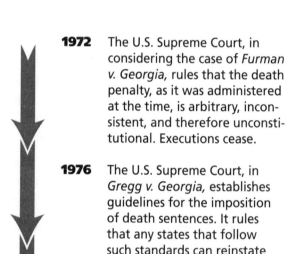

1972 The U.S. Supreme Court, in considering the case of *Furman v. Georgia,* rules that the death penalty, as it was administered at the time, is arbitrary, inconsistent, and therefore unconstitutional. Executions cease.

1976 The U.S. Supreme Court, in *Gregg v. Georgia,* establishes guidelines for the imposition of death sentences. It rules that any states that follow such standards can reinstate the death penalty.

1976 Canada abolishes the death penalty.

1977 Gary Gilmore is killed by firing squad in Utah. He's the first person executed in the modern era of U.S. capital punishment.

1977 Delbert Tibbs is the first person exonerated in the modern era of U.S. capital punishment.

1985 Australia abolishes the death penalty.

1987 The Supreme Court's decision in *McCleskey v. Kemp* identifies, but proposes no steps to rectify racial discrepancies in the application of the death penalty.

1992 Barry Scheck and Peter Neufeld found the first Innocence Project at Benjamin N. Cardozo School of Law, New York.

1993 In *Herrera v. Collins,* the U.S. Supreme Court rules that there is no inherent right to a federal hearing for inmates who have missed the statutory cutoff date in their state, even where there is new evidence alleging actual innocence.

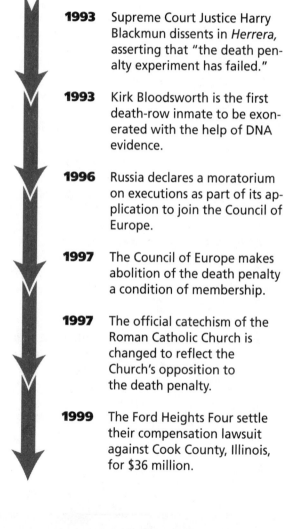

1993   Supreme Court Justice Harry Blackmun dissents in *Herrera,* asserting that "the death penalty experiment has failed."

1993   Kirk Bloodsworth is the first death-row inmate to be exonerated with the help of DNA evidence.

1996   Russia declares a moratorium on executions as part of its application to join the Council of Europe.

1997   The Council of Europe makes abolition of the death penalty a condition of membership.

1997   The official catechism of the Roman Catholic Church is changed to reflect the Church's opposition to the death penalty.

1999   The Ford Heights Four settle their compensation lawsuit against Cook County, Illinois, for $36 million.

2002 The U.S. Supreme Court, in *Atkins v. Virginia,* rules that it is unconstitutional to execute a mentally retarded individual.

2003 Governor George Ryan pardons or commutes to life in prison every convict on Illinois's death row.

2003 Louisiana's John Thompson is acquitted and becomes the 100th man exonerated from death row in the modern era of capital punishment (since 1977).

2004 The United States ranks fourth in the list of countries with the most executions in this year, behind China, Iran, and Vietnam.

2004 California rules that the death penalty is unconstitutional.

2004 Kansas rules that the death penalty is unconstitutional.

2005 The March 2005 U.S. Supreme
Court decision in *Roper v. Sim-mons* rules that it is unconstitutional to execute any person
who was a juvenile (under the
age of 18) at the time of commission of the capital crime.

2005 On December 2, 2005, Kenneth
Boyd is the 1,000th person
executed in the modern era
of the U.S. death penalty.
He was put to death by
lethal injection in North
Carolina. On the same day,
Shawn Humphries became the
1,001st person to be executed
when he was killed by lethal
injection in South Carolina.

Amazing Facts and Figures

- The number of new prisoners on death row has fallen for the last four years because the murder rate in the United States is at its lowest in 40 years. (Bureau of Justice Statistics report)

- California, Florida, and Texas together account for 44 percent of the nation's death-row population.

- As of December 31, 2004, there were 3,315 people on death row.

- The 59 inmates executed in 2004 had spent an average of 11 years on death row. Of those executed, 36 were white, 19 African-American, 3 Hispanic, and 1 Asian. One inmate was electrocuted; the rest were put to death by lethal injection.

- Fifteen death-row inmates have been exonerated by the use of DNA tests in the United States.

- In the 25 years from 1973 to 1998, there were an average 2.96 exonerations per year. In the five years 1998 through 2003, that average has risen to 7.60 exonerations. (Death Penalty Information Center)

U.S. EXECUTIONS IN 2004 BY STATE

Texas	23
Ohio	7
Oklahoma	6
Virginia	5
North Carolina	4
South Carolina	4
Alabama	2
Florida	2
Georgia	2
Nevada	2
Arkansas	1
Maryland	1

Source: Bureau of Justice Statistics

INTERNET RESOURCES

Amnesty International • www.amnesty.org

Canadian Coaltion Against the Death Penalty • www.ccadp.org

Death Penalty Information Center • www.deathpenaltyinfo.org

Death Penalty Law Review Center • www.law-forensic.com/dp_law_review_center.htm

Pro Death Penalty • www.pro-deathpenalty.com

EXECUTIONS BY STATE SINCE 1976

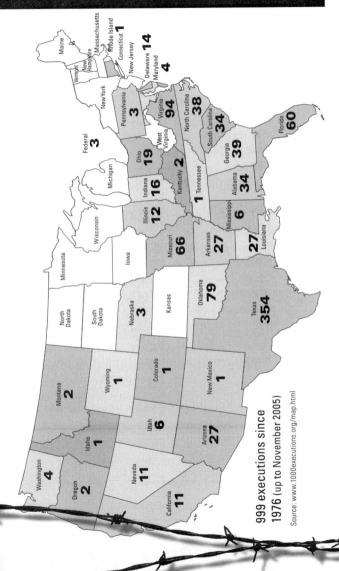

999 executions since 1976 (up to November 2005)

Source: www.1000executions.org/map.html

THOSE EXONERATED FROM DEATH ROW SINCE 1976

Thomas Gladish	NM	1976	Robert Cox	FL	198?
Richard Greer	NM	1976	Timothy Hennis	NC	198?
Ronald Keine	NM	1976	James Richardson	FL	198?
Clarence Smith	NM	1976	Clarence Brandley	TX	199?
Delbert Tibbs	FL	1977	John C. Skelton	TX	199?
Earl Charles	GA	1978	Dale Johnston	OH	199?
Jonathan Treadway	AZ	1978	Jimmy Lee Mathers	AZ	1990
Gary Beeman	OH	1979	Gary Nelson	GA	199?
Jerry Banks	GA	1980	Bradley P. Scott	FL	199?
Larry Hicks	IN	1980	Charles Smith	IN	199?
Charles Ray Giddens	OK	1981	Jay C. Smith	PA	1992
Michael Linder	SC	1981	Kirk Bloodsworth	MD	199?
Johnny Ross	LA	1981	Federico M. Macias	TX	199?
Ernest (Shuhaa) Graham	CA	1981	Walter McMillian	AL	199?
Annibal Jaramillo	FL	1982	Gregory R. Wilhoit	OK	199?
Lawyer Johnson	MA	1982	James Robison	AZ	199?
Larry Fisher	MS	1985	Muneer Deeb	TX	199?
Anthony Brown	FL	1986	Andrew Golden	FL	199?
Neil Ferber	PA	1986	Joseph Burrows	IL	199?
Clifford Henry Bowen	OK	1986	Adolph Munson	OK	199?
Joseph Green Brown	FL	1987	Robert Charles Cruz	AZ	199?
Perry Cobb	IL	1987	Rolando Cruz	IL	199?
Darby (Williams) Tillis	IL	1987	Alejandro Hernandez	IL	199?
Vernon McManus	TX	1987	Sabrina Butler	MS	199?
Anthony Ray Peek	FL	1987	Verneal Jimerson	IL	199?
Juan Ramos	FL	1987	Dennis Williams	IL	199?
Robert Wallace	GA	1987	Roberto Miranda	NV	199?
Richard Neal Jones	OK	1987	Gary Gauger	IL	199?
Willie Brown	FL	1988	Troy Lee Jones	CA	199?
Larry Troy	FL	1988	Carl Lawson	IL	199?
Randall Dale Adams	TX	1989	David Wayne Grannis	AZ	199?

THOSE EXONERATED FROM DEATH ROW SINCE 1976

Name	State	Year
icardo Aldape Guerra	TX	1997
enjamin Harris	WA	1997
obert Hayes	FL	1997
hristopher McCrimmon	AZ	1997
andall Padgett	AL	1997
ames Bo Cochran	AL	1997
obert Lee Miller, Jr.	OK	1998
urtis Kyles	LA	1998
hareef Cousin	LA	1999
nthony Porter	IL	1999
teven Smith	IL	1999
onald Williamson	OK	1999
onald Jones	IL	1999
larence Dexter, Jr.	MO	1999
Varren Douglas Manning	SC	1999
lfred Rivera	NC	1999
teve Manning	IL	2000
ric Clemmons	MO	2000
oseph Nahume Green	FL	2000
arl Washington	VA	2000
Villiam Nieves	PA	2000
rank Lee Smith*	FL	2000
lichael Graham	LA	2000
lbert Burrell	LA	2000
scar Lee Morris	CA	2000
eter Limone	MA	2001
ary Drinkard	AL	2001
oaquin Jose Martinez	FL	2001
eremy Sheets	NE	2001
harles Fain	ID	2001
uan Roberto Melendez	FL	2002
Ray Krone	AZ	2002
Thomas Kimbell, Jr.	PA	2002
Larry Osborne	KY	2002
Aaron Patterson	IL	2003
Madison Hobley	IL	2003
Leroy Orange	IL	2003
Stanley Howard	IL	2003
Rudolph Holton	FL	2003
Lemuel Prion	AZ	2003
Wesley Quick	AL	2003
John Thompson	LA	2003
Timothy Howard	OH	2003
Gary Lamar James	OH	2003
Joseph Amrine	MO	2003
Nicholas Yarris	PA	2003
Alan Gell	NC	2004
Gordon Steid	IL	2004
Laurence Adams	MA	2004
Dan L. Bright	LA	2004
Ryan Matthews	LA	2004
Ernest Ray Willis	TX	2004
Derrick Jamison	OH	2005
Harold Wilson	PA	2005

*exonerated after dying of cancer
 on death row

What Others Say

"If statistics are any indication, the system may well be allowing some innocent defendants to be executed."

Recently retired Supreme Court Justice Sandra Day O'Connor

"Perhaps the bleakest fact of all is that the death penalty is imposed not only in a freakish and discriminatory manner, but also in some cases upon defendants who are actually innocent."

Supreme Court Justice William J. Brennan Jr., 1994

"You always lose some soldiers in any war."

Senator David Jaye, R-Washington Township, commenting on the risk of executing an innocent person

"Don't kill for me."

*Slogan for the "1000 Executions"
anti-death-penalty campaign*

"One searches in vain for the
execution of any members of
the affluent strata of our society."

Supreme Court Justice William Douglas

"The death penalty is the
privilege of the poor!"

*Clinton Duffy, former warden
of San Quentin Prison*

"When God forbids us to kill, he not only
prohibits the violence that is condemned
by public laws, but he also forbids the
violence that is deemed lawful by men."

*Lanctantius, The Divine Institute,
Book 6, Chapter 20*

"I feel morally and intellectually obligated simply to concede that the death penalty experiment has failed."

Supreme Court Justice Harry Blackmun, in his dissenting opinion in Callins v. James (1994)

"If what were at issue here was the fabrication of toasters ... or the processing of social security claims, or the pre-takeoff inspection of commercial aircraft, or the conduct of any other private- or public-sector activity—neither the consuming and the taxpaying public, nor managers and investors, would for a moment tolerate the error-rates and attendant costs that dozens of states and the nation as a whole have tolerated in their capital punishment system for decades. Any system with this much error and expense would be halted immediately, examined, and either reformed or scrapped."

James Liebman

Bibliography

Books

Cohen, Stanley. *The Wrong Men: America's Epidemic of Wrongful Death Row Convictions.* Carroll & Graf Publishers: New York, 2003.

Galliher, John F., Larry W. Koch, David Patrick Keys, and Teresa J. Guess. *America Without the Death Penalty: States Leading the Way.* Northeastern University Press: Boston, 2002.

Jackson, Rev. Jesse L. Sr., Jesse L. Jackson Jr., and Bruce Shapiro. *Legal Lynching: The Death Penalty and America's Future.* The New Press: New York, 2001.

Johnson, Robert. *Death Work: A Study of the Modern Execution Process.* Brooks/Cole Publisher: Pacific Grove, CA, 1990.

Kurtis, Bill. *The Death Penalty on Trial: Crisis in American Justice.* Public Affairs (Perseus Books Group): New York, 2004.

Prejean, Sister Helen. *The Death of Innocents: An Eyewitness Account of Wrongful Executions.* Random House: New York, 2005.

Prejean, Sister Helen. *Dead Man Walking: An Eyewitness Account of the Death Penalty in the United States.* Vintage Books: New York, 1993.

Protess, David and Rob Warden. *A Promise of Justice: The Eighteen-Year Fight to Save Four Innocent Men.* Hyperion Books: New York, 1998.

Radelet, Michael L., Hugo Adam Bedau, and Constance E. Putnam. *In Spite of Innocence: Erroneous Convictions in Capital Cases.* Northeastern University Press: Boston, 1994.

Scheck, Barry, Peter Neufeld, and Jim Dwyer. *Actual Innocence: Five Days to Execution, and Other Dispatches from the Wrongfully Convicted.* Doubleday: New York, 2000.

Articles and Studies

American Civil Liberties Union. "DNA Testing and the Death Penalty." 2002. Available from: http://www.aclu.org/capital/innocence/10392pub20020626.html.

Amnesty International USA. "Fatal Flaws: Innocence and the Death Penalty in the United States." 1998. http://web.amnesty.org/library/Index/engAMR510691998.

Bedau, Hugo Adam and Michael L. Radelet. "The Myth of Infallibility: A Reply to Markman and Cassell." *Stanford Law Review* 41 (1988): 161–170.

Death Penalty Information Center. "Innocence and the Crisis in the American Death Penalty." Report prepared by Richard C. Dieter, Executive Director. Washington, DC; 2004.

Ellsworth, Phoebe C. and Lee Ross. "Public Opinion and Capital Punishment: A Close Examination of the Views of Abolitionists and Retentionists." *Crime and Delinquency* 29 (1983):116–169.

Florida Commission on Capital Cases. "Case Histories: A Review of 24 Individuals Released from Death Row." Locke Burt, Chairman; 2002.

Gross, Samuel R., Kristen Jacoby, Daniel J. Matheson, Nicholas Montgomery, and Sujata Patil. "Exonerations in the United States 1989 through 2003." *Journal of Criminal Law and Criminology* 95 (2). Northwestern University School of Law; 2005.

Honeyman, Jennifer C. and James R.P. Ogloff. "Capital Punishment: Arguments for Life and Death." *Canadian Journal of Behavioural Science* 28 (January 1996).

Liebman, James. "A Broken System: Error Rates in Capital Cases, 1973–1995." Report prepared for the U.S. Senate Committee on the Judiciary, 2000.

Montgomery, L. "Md. Questioning Local Extremes on Death Penalty." *Washington Post,* May 12, 2002.